WHAT WE CAN LEARN FROM

Hinduism

Rediscovering the mystical

Marcus Braybrooke

WHAT WE CAN LEARN FROM

Hinduism

Rediscovering the mystical

Marcus Braybrooke

ISBN 1 903816-20-3

Design: Nautilus Design (UK) Ltd

Write to:

John Hunt Publishing Ltd
46A West Street
Alresford
Hampshire SO24 9AU
UK

A CIP catalogue record for this book is available from the British Library.

Printed in the UK by Ashford Colour Press Ltd, Gosport, Hants

Visit us on the Web at: www.o-books.net

CONTENTS

For Jeremy and Amanda,

who devote their lives to seeking the health of other people

PREFACE

My first book, *Together to the Truth*, which was published thirty years ago, was a comparative study of modern Christianity and modern Hinduism. I was glad, therefore, when John Hunt gave me the opportunity to reflect again about the relationship of Hinduism and Christianity. This is a much more personal book than *Together to the Truth* and serves as an acknowledgment of the enrichment that Hindu friends and Hindu beliefs and practices have brought to my life.

I am grateful to John Hunt and to all his colleagues. I am also very grateful to Professor Seshagiri Rao and Professor Hal French for reading the script and for writing forewords and also to Mary and to Sandy and Jael Bharat of the International Inter-faith Centre for reading the script and for their helpful advice. I once again express my thanks to Mary for her patience with me, even allowing me to make final corrections while we were on holiday, and for so often travelling with me to India.

The book is dedicated to our son Jeremy and our daughter-in-law Amanda, who spent their honeymoon in India. Jeremy has stayed at Fr Bede Griffiths' ashram and encouraged me to go there too and he and Amanda shared in the breathtaking World Congress of Faiths tour to Tibet.

I hope this book will make some small contribution to greater mutual appreciation between members of two great spiritual traditions and increase fellowship and compassion, which the bombing of Afghanistan, taking place as I write, suggests is in all too short supply.

Marcus Braybrooke
Marbesa Spain October 2001

FOREWORD

by
Hal French
Distinguished Professor Emeritus, Department of Religious Studies, University of South Carolina

This new book by Marcus Braybrooke continues his extensive exploration into relations between different world faiths, all designed to deepen our understanding and appreciation of each. A particular strength of this volume, which engages in 'Rethinking Theology', is that it is clearly cast in the mould of experiential theology. His conclusions are profusely illustrated with his own rich, on-site encounters with expressions of Hinduism and the related faiths of India. But his own, personally acquired, positions are buttressed as well by two intellectual streams, Hindu philosophy and Western idealism.

A pervasive question, growing logically out of Braybrooke's immersion in inter-faith concerns, is the one that asks whether our different spiritual paths may lead to the same God. Ramakrishna's many-faceted *sadhana* (spiritual path) is cited in support of the conviction that this is so, and Bede Griffiths, who emerges as perhaps the author's most influential source, encourages us, by that insight, to regard each other as fellow pilgrims.

The limitations of language and logic refute claims by any tradition to possession of absolute truth, which so often relativizes competing truth claims of others. In India, the 'Neti, neti,' ('not this, not that') disavowals, which follow any purported assertions about reality, indicate that Hindu philosophy holds an implicit self-critique, even of its most cherished postulates. This is matched in the West, as Braybrooke notes, with philosophers such as Wittgenstein, whose extensive investigations into the limitations of language nevertheless point to a reality beyond it, much in the same manner as Zen suggests the image of a finger, which is not the moon, points beyond itself to the moon. We are not, in our different traditions, given the luxury of blueprints of reality, but the sharing of mystical glimpses provides us with incentives for further explorations.

Again, this supports the necessity of listening to each other, learning from each other. Hinduism's record of openness to such dialogue, within and beyond its own largely borderless parameters, provides a very useful model for our more self-contained western traditions.

Among the different strands of faith, which support alternative mystical approaches, Braybrooke notes in particular the contributions of both theistic and trans-personal sources in Hinduism. While he states his own preference for the theistic, he gives extensive attention, as well, to monistic philosophies, which aspire to union, not merely communion, with the divine. Similarly, while within theistic expressions his own stated preference is for simplicity, he details, with genuine sympathy, the assumptions behind the colourful rituals and images that are so characteristic of Hindu theism. Beyond the pejorative term, 'idols', the meaning to the worshipper is examined. One thinks, in this connection, of the Hindu term *arca* (material image), which assumes that the intention of the devotee in fashioning the image is met with the eagerness of the divine to inhabit it for the devotional benefit of the devotee.

There is much more. The author credits Jainism as one of the root systems inspiring Gandhi's fidelity to *ahimsa* or non-violence. And while Braybrooke identifies himself as a vegetarian and a pacifist, he notes that Sikhism, which began in a very quietistic and pacifistic mode, had to modify that stance because of historical necessity. Thus Braybrooke recognizes the necessity to qualify our positions, not defending them dogmatically or proselytizing others in the name of non-negotiable postulates.

All of this lends itself to an enhanced awareness of what Hinduism can bring to the dialogue. The mystical wealth that it offers, grounded alike in philosophical inquiry, in devotional richness, and in ethical expression, challenges 'fellow pilgrims' on other paths to turn aside and see how these grace notes may enhance our own journey.

FOREWORD

by
Seshagiri Rao
Professor Emeritus of the University of Virginia
and Chief Editor of the Encyclopedia of Hinduism

The author, known for his ecumenical writings, adopts in this book a new approach to the study of the world's religions. Holding the great faiths as part of the religious history of humanity, he endeavours to gather fruits of the spirit from any or all of them, and in this case Hinduism. His approach is bold, human and experiential. In the author's view, religious categories such as ritual and liturgy, dogma and doctrine are secondary to experience, and they are frequently divisive. Experience of the Divine, on the other hand, creates a sense of oneness with all humans and a concern for the poor, the sick and the suffering. Focusing on the positive insights, values and practices of Hinduism, he demonstrates in an existential way, their influences on his own life and thought, especially how they helped him to discover the mystical heart of Christianity.

The book draws our attention to some valuable Hindu contributions to humanity's understanding of the spiritual world. It substantiates that world religions, in co-operation with one another, can do a great deal to rehabilitate humanity, by giving it meaning and purpose. It represents a new trend in religious studies. It deserves wide attention.

Introduction

Hinduism can help Christians in the West rediscover a sense of the mystical - an awareness of the reality of the Divine, who or which can never adequately be described in human language. Hinduism can serve as a mirror to help Christians recover their mystical traditions and thereby help the Church to communicate with people today at the level of experience rather than doctrine.

To explain a little more what I mean by the mystical - a term I shall use quite often in this book - let me quote a passage that I wrote for a collection of personal testimonies entitled *Glimpses of God*. I describe a visit to the ashram in South India of Fr Bede Griffiths, who explored the relationship of Hindu and Christian mysticism.

> At first the physical discomfort of sitting cross-legged on the floor, sleeping on a hard board and readapting to an Indian way of life made concentration difficult. The friendship of others at the ashram helped me to relax. Then walks beside the great holy river Cauvery at sunset and sunrise renewed the 'sense of presence' - an awareness of the scale of the universe and my humble place in it - and a sense of peace and stillness. I felt as if I were able to relax in a warm ocean of love and that my worries and insecurity were gently washed away. I thought of my mother dying of cancer and knew that she, too, would soon be free from physical discomfort and humiliation, relaxing in the same ocean of love.
>
> Then, at the Eucharist, which incorporated so much of the Hindu temple ritual, the celebrant called us to communion with the words, 'Jesus invites us all to share in God's limitless love.' The sense of presence became the experience of

overwhelming love and acceptance. I recognized that my moments of panic, of defensiveness and of aggressiveness came from feelings of not being able to cope. But what did it matter if God wanted to make a fool of me? I was loved without reserve - all I needed was to lean on the love of God, which is always available. I sensed that this limitless love of God embraces all people and indeed the whole of creation.

Neither experience was new. I have often sensed 'the presence' in nature, most intensely in the desert of Sinai and in the outback of Australia, but also in the beauty that surrounds us everywhere in nature. I have long known the forgiving and accepting love of Jesus, even if, almost as often, I forget it. The Cross has always been for me the symbol of that total accepting love of God made known in Christ - a love shown in Jesus' concern for the poor and outcast. At each communion service I have been renewed in that love which the Cross communicates.

What was new was that, beside the Cauvery river, the 'presence' of mystery in nature and the revelation in Jesus of infinite love and peace were united. And sensing that love, I felt renewed compassion for other people and for all living beings.[1]

Compared to an experience of the reality of the Divine, debates about doctrine and reform of ritual and liturgy are comparatively unimportant and the struggle of the institutional church to reinvent itself is irrelevant.

To define God is to limit that which is unlimited and infinite. All religious language should be tentative and provisional. It should never, therefore, be the cause of division. Mystical vision helps us to see ourselves as part of a spiritual fellowship that knows no barriers.

It also creates in us a sense of our oneness with all other people and with all life and so it inspires empathy for the poor and a concern to break down the unjust structures of society. It fills us also with compassion for all living beings. Thereby, mystic vision offers, I believe, genuine hope for the transformation of our world society and renewal of spiritual life.

As I was coming to an end of writing this book, I came across the advice given by Henri de Lubac, author of a classic study on Catholicism, to Fr Jules Monchanin, one of the founders of the Shantivanam Ashram where Fr Bede Griffiths made his home, 'to rethink everything in terms of theology, and to rethink theology in terms of mysticism.'[2]

Fr Bede Griffiths first went to India in 1956, but it was not until 1968 that he settled at Shantivanam. I first went to India in 1962 and Bede Griffiths' *Christian Ashram*, published in 1966, was one of the few books I found which resonated with my first hesitant attempts to discover a more universal expression of Christianity. I have been deeply influenced by Fr Bede Griffiths both as a person and a writer. In writing this book, I had, however, not recently reread his writings, but as this book was nearing completion, I read Judson B. Trapnell's new study of Bede Griffiths.[3] The various quotations from Fr Bede in this book were added at this stage. I mention this because it suggests I am not alone in having been helped by Hinduism to discover the mystical heart of Christianity.

There are many others who have been influenced in this way. Let Brother Wayne Teasdale, who was deeply influenced by time spent in India and who was initiated by Fr Bede in the way of *sannyasa*, the way of renunciation and dedication to God, serve as an example. In his book *The Mystic Heart*, Brother Wayne develops a genuine and comprehensive spirituality that draws on the mystical core of the world's great religions.[4] He ends his book with these words,

> Spirituality is the very breath of the inner life. It is an essential resource in the transformation of consciousness on our planet, and it will be enormously beneficial in our attempts to build a new universal society. Spirituality ... is the quality that we most require in our time and in the ages to come, but it is a quality refined only in the mystic heart, in the steady cultivation of compassion and love that risks all for the sake of others. It is these resources that we desperately need as we build the civilization with a heart, a universal society capable of embracing all that is, putting it to service in the transformation of the world. May the mystics lead the way to this rebirth of the human community that will harmonize itself with the cosmos and finally make peace with all beings.[5]

The sense that spiritual renewal in the West will come from a rediscovery of the mystic heart of religion is not new. F. C. Happold, for example, in his *Religious Faith and Twentieth-Century Man*, published in 1966, spoke of the mystical 'as as a way out of the spiritual dilemma of modern man.'[6] Many individuals have found this to be true by exploring Eastern religions or joining New Religious Movements. As Jacob Needleman noted in 1970 'the contemporary disillusionment with religion has revealed itself to be a *religious* disillusionment. Men are moving away from the forms and trappings of Judaism and Christianity not because they have stopped searching for transcendental answers to the fundamental questions of human life, but because that search has now intensified beyond measure.'[7]

I myself have found lasting spiritual sustenance in Christianity. I recognize that the growth of the evangelical and charismatic traditions in the churches reflects a similar longing for religious experience. But I cannot accept the narrowness of their theology, as I have also drunk from the wellsprings of other religions, especially Hinduism and Judaism. Both have helped me rethink my understanding of Christianity and in this book I explore the influence of Hinduism.

This is not another 'Introduction to Hinduism.' When I first went to India I was told by Fr Murray Rogers, who founded a Christian ashram near Bareilly, that the external dialogue has to be accompanied by an internal dialogue. By this he meant that as one learns about another faith, either by reading or conversation, one then reflects on this in an inner dialogue with the Lord. In this book I share some of my inner dialogue, which is why this has to be a personal account and why, despite the emphasis on my growing awareness of the mystical, I reflect on some other matters.

I recognize that Hinduism is immensely varied. Indeed the word is one imposed by Europeans on the religious life of India. Other people will have experienced different dimensions of Hinduism. Hinduism is not confined to India and I have learned from Hindus in other parts of the world. Hinduism, moreover, is not the only religion in India and it has seemed right to make some reference to what I have gained from talking to some members of other faiths there.

Christianity too, of course, is also very varied and maybe these religious labels will continue to lose their meaning in the twenty-first century. My hope is that this book will encourage other Christians to make a similar journey and discover the spiritual enrichment that is offered to us by a deeper awareness of some of India's religious traditions.

All the great faiths hold in trust sacred treasures, which are the spiritual heritage of humankind. These need to be unlocked from the doctrines and rituals which too often imprison them so that as we sense our oneness with the Divine Reality we shall feel that we are one with all other people and be filled with a universal compassion which can transform the injustice and suffering in the world.

---

[1] From a chapter in *Glimpses of God*, ed. D. Cohn-Sherbok, Duckworth, 1994, pp. 74-76.
[2] Quoted by J. B. Trapnell in *Bede Griffiths: A Life in Dialogue*, State University of New York Press, 2001. p. 155. He refers to the quotation of this phrase by Bede Griffiths in *The Cosmic Revelation: The Hindu Way to God*, Templegate Publishers, Illinois, 1983, p. 85.
[3] J. B. Trapnell, *Bede Griffiths: A Life in Dialogue*, State University of New York Press, 2001.
[4] W. Teasdale, *The Mystic Heart*, New World Library, Novato, California, 1999.
[5] W. Teasdale, *The Mystic Heart*, New World Library, Novato, California, 1999, pp. 249-250.
[6] F. C. Happold, *Religious Faith and Twentieth-Century Man*, Penguin, 1966, p. 7.
[7] J. Needleman, *The New Religions*, Allen Lane, The Penguin Press, 1970, p. xi.

THE DIVINE MYSTERY: 'NOT THIS, NOT THAT'

Almost as soon as I had finished studying theology at Cambridge, I was on my way to India. I did not stop to collect my degree in person. Instead, I wanted to reach Tambaram in time to start the summer term and my year at Madras Christian College. There, thanks to a World Council of Churches' scholarship, I had the opportunity in an unstructured way to learn about Hinduism and Indian philosophy.

In the early sixties, world religions were not taught in schools and, apart from Oriental studies, they were seldom taught at universities. In Cambridge, Dr A. C. Bouquet, an Anglican priest and pioneer student of 'comparative religion', offered a course, but it was timetabled for 5.00 p.m. in the summer term, just before the main examinations, and I was not surprised that only four other students had enrolled for the course.

Time spent in North Africa during my National Service and a visit to Israel sparked an interest in Islam and Judaism. The fascination with world religions was stimulated by preparatory reading for a conference arranged for young people who saw themselves as potential missionaries. Each of the speakers was keen to search, below superficial differences, for the deeper meeting points of religions. They included Kenneth Cragg, a sympathetic and very knowledgeable writer on Islam, George Appleton, who had worked in Burma for many years where he developed a love and respect for Buddhism and who was later to be Anglican Archbishop in Jerusalem, and Dr Basu, a Hindu scholar at Durham University, who spoke about two creative twentieth-century thinkers, Aurobindo and Teilhard de Chardin.

It is hard now, forty years later, to remember the impact of the first weeks in India. Certainly I recall the humidity and the delight in the cool stillness of the early morning. I had to adjust to the food and to the way of life in an Indian student hostel - although almost at once I was taken out to buy a bed as it was assumed that unlike my fellow students a 'white man' could not sleep on the floor!

But perhaps intellectually the first surprise was that the reality of God was taken for granted. I am not just thinking of the images of divine beings that are omni-present, but the philosophic acceptance of spiritual knowledge. Horst Georg Pöhlmann, writing of his first visit to India in 1989, says, 'Religion is practised as a matter of course; people pay brief visits to the temple between their shopping ... Everyone in the street can see through the open temple door the sacred fire which burns in the dark sanctuary of the temple before the image of God ... There is no distinction between the sacred and the profane, between religion and everyday, as with us. Here God really is a God of the everyday. Religion is something natural ... It is an innermost need ... There is no secularization. Everyone is religious. Among the Hindus every house, every shop, every rickshaw has the picture of a deity.'[1]

The situation in the sixties was more ambiguous. Recently Indian religious communities have affirmed their identity - often over against other groups - by building new temples or restoring old ones. In the sixties the humanism and socialism of Pandit Nehru was still influential and perhaps the majority of students at Madras Christian College, except for the committed Christians, put their trust in Western values rather than traditional religious beliefs, although this was probably not true of students at the Hindu Vivekananda College, where I attended some lectures. In the West too, many people assumed the role of religion would continue to decline in the modern world.

1963 saw the publication of John Robinson's *Honest to God*, of which I first heard in a one-paragraph report in an Indian newspaper, and of Paul van Buren's *The Secular Meaning of the Gospel.* Both writers acknowledged their debt to Dietrich Bonhoeffer, who was put to death by the Nazis. In his letters from prison he wrote of the world 'coming of age.' By this he meant that people no longer believed in a transcendent realm and did not require God as an explanation of what happened in the world. 'Honesty demands,' wrote Bonhoeffer, 'that we recognize that we live in the world as if there were no God.'[2] 'People feel that they can get along perfectly well without religion,' said John Robinson and added that 'Bonhoeffer's answer was to say that God is deliberately calling us in this twentieth century to a form of Christianity that does not depend upon the premise of religion.'[3]

At the same time, there was growing interest in Rudolf Bultmann's call to 'demythologize' the gospel.[4] He claimed that whereas New Testament writers assumed divine intervention in history, such a belief was unintelligible to modern man and that the entire conception of a supernatural order, which invades and perforates this one, must be abandoned. It was argued that in a secular age people no longer believed in divine intervention or activity. For example, miracles could be given a 'scientific' explanation and few people spoke of natural disasters as 'the judgement of God.' 'But if so,' asked Robinson, 'what do we mean by God, by revelation, and what becomes of Christianity?'[5] These ideas stimulated what became known as 'Death of God' theology. It was claimed that the idea of a transcendent God was outmoded, although writers differed on whether the image of God had to go or whether there was no God of whom to speak.

At the same time the questioning of the language and indeed of the reality of God was central to the study of religious philosophy in most British universities. Religious language was under scrutiny from a school of philosophy known as 'Linguistic Analysis'. In part, this was an attempt to answer the accusation of A. J. Ayer, a leading Logical Empiricist, that religious and theological expressions are without literal significance because there is no way in which they can be verified or falsified. Religious language, Ayer claimed, is entirely emotive and lacks all cognitive value. Linguistic analysts examined the way in which religious statements are actually used. They appear to make factual claims, for example, that after the Resurrection Jesus ascended into heaven, whereas this may be a coded way of expressing the hope that 'Love is the strongest power in the universe.' Religious belief was regarded as only an expression of intent to act in a certain ethical way. Religion was about how to behave and not about how to relate to a Divine Reality.

Suddenly to be immersed in Indian religious thinking, which assumes the existence of a Divine reality and that union with the Divine (*moksa*) is the goal of the spiritual quest, was liberating and refreshing. There are in classical Hinduism three recognized paths (*sadhanas*) to God: the way of disinterested service of others, the way of devotion and the way of knowledge (*karma-yoga, bhakti-yoga* and *jnana-yoga*). The word *yoga*, which is cognate with the English word 'yoke', means union with God and the way to that union. The third path, *jnana*, means spiritual insight rather than intellectual knowledge. There are two kinds of knowledge: one is the result of the study of the scriptures, but the other is realization or experience of union with the Divine. Intellectual knowledge is not enough. In the *Chandogya Upanishad*, the student Narada complains, 'I have studied all the Vedas, grammar, the sciences and the fine arts, but I have not known the Self and so I am in sorrow.'[6] Another conceited young student, Svetaketu, is asked by his father, 'As you consider yourself so well-read ... have you ever asked for that instruction by which we hear what cannot be heard, by which we perceive what cannot be perceived, by which we know what cannot be known?'[7]

Spiritual intuition - the experience of the Divine - is accepted in Hindu philosophy as a valid source of knowledge. This confirmed my feelings that the presuppositions of linguistic philosophy were too limited. Indeed the philosopher Ludwig Wittgenstein, who exposed the limitations of our use of language, himself said, as my Hindu professor at Madras Christian College told me, that there was a mystery beyond language. 'Whereof one cannot speak, thereof one must keep silent.'[8]

For me this Hindu emphasis on experience of the Divine reinforced my own basic conviction. If I was asked to summarize my deepest spiritual aspiration, I would use the words of St Paul, 'It is no longer I that live, but Christ Jesus lives in me,'[9] or I would echo the yearning from the Prayer of Humble Access in the Book of Common Prayer that 'I might evermore dwell in Christ and he in me.' My faith was rooted in spiritual or mystical experience. Learning about Hindu philosophy and Western Idealist philosophers, such as Royce and Bosanquet, to whom my Indian professor Dr C. T. K. Chari introduced me, gave me an intellectual basis for a theology rooted in religious experience.

Let me clarify what I mean by religious experience by quoting from William James' landmark book, *The Varieties of Religious Experience,* which was first published in 1902. He puts clearly what I had myself sensed and for which I was discovering an intellectual basis in those first months of being immersed in Hindu philosophy.

> The overcoming of all the usual barriers between the individual and the Absolute is the great mystic achievement. In mystic states we become one with the Absolute and we

> become aware of our oneness. This is the everlasting and triumphant mystical tradition, hardly altered by differences of clime and creed. In Hinduism, in Sufism, in Christian mysticism, ... we find the same recurring note, so that there is about mystical utterances an eternal unanimity which ought to make a critic stop and think, and which brings it about that the mystical classics have, as has been said, neither birthday nor native land. Perpetually telling of the unity of man with God, their speech antedates language, and they do not grow old.[10]

The mystic experience is a sense of oneness with All Being - whether that is described as God, Nature or the Real. The experience cannot be adequately expressed in words. Although in Hinduism, many facets of the One Divine Being are pictured as gods, Hindu teachers have always made clear that there is only one Spiritual Reality. Brahman is the One Reality which is the Ground and Principle of all beings. Brahman is described as Being, Consciousness and Bliss (*Sat, Cit, Ananda*). Brahman cannot be described. '*Neti, Neti*, Not this, not that.' Hinduism can remind us of the holiness and wonder of a God who is beyond our imagining. It recalls the so-called 'apophatic' tradition in Christian thinking that God, 'The Cloud of Unknowing', is greater than any picture we have of the Divine. God is best spoken of in negative terms, as in the hymn

> Immortal, invisible God only wise,
> In light inaccessible hid from our eyes.

As the fourth-century Greek father, Gregory of Nazianzus (c. 329 - c. 389), asked, 'By what name shall we name you, you who are beyond all name?'[11]

Many Indian religious teachers remind us of the limitations of our language but at the same time they insist that we can sense our oneness with God, who is found in the very depth of our being. It is said that the soul or *atman* is one with *Brahman*. In Christian mystical tradition there is the same emphasis on discovering God as our deepest inner reality. The medieval mystic Meister Eckhart said, 'the soul is nearer to God than it is to the body which makes us human.' George Fox, the founder of the Quakers, spoke of the inner light, which he identified with the living Christ. Incidentally, he said he discovered this inner light, 'experimentally, without the help of any man, book or writing.'

The emphasis on religious experience means also that in seeking to commend Christianity to others I have tried to start from people's often half-glimpsed awareness of a deeper dimension to life.

Recently I have been writing an introductory book, *Learn to Pray*. It is intended for people who have never prayed and may not see themselves as religious. The editors and I had long discussions about whether to use the word God. Would it put people off even before they started to read the book? A recent survey showed that the majority of people questioned pictured God as 'an old man with a long white beard up in the sky.' It was not surprising that many of them also said that they did not believe in God.

Theology may have moved on from the 'God is dead' phase of the sixties, but to many in the West the language of religion and even more the reality of spiritual experience is still alien. A recent survey claimed that among a group of young people who called themselves Christian, forty five per cent said they did not believe in God.[12] Christians who wish to encourage others to grow in faith have first to help people be aware of a deeper dimension to life. The mystery of a child's birth, a near-death experience, the beauty of a sunset - all these can make us aware that there is more to life than material existence. The occasional sense of the 'timeless moment' should be a threshold to the deeper mysteries of faith. To many people, however, the Church appears to offer pre-packaged answers which do not match their experience of life or their need.

One reason why, especially in the seventies and eighties, a number of people in the West turned to Eastern religions, was I think because they offered spiritual experience. Talking to a number of Europeans and Americans who have joined Hindu religious movements, all have said that they discovered in them a spiritual experience that they had not found in Christianity. Scripture and worship, 'like fingers pointing to the moon', should lead us beyond themselves and I have come to find the way of silence and contemplation often more helpful than elaborate and wordy worship.

How far the renewed interest of some Christians in the mystical and contemplative traditions is indebted to Hinduism it is hard to say, but Western Christians can still be helped to discover a deeper dimension to life by encounter with the authentic spiritual teaching and practice of Hinduism.

---

[1] H. G. Pöhlmann, *Encounters with Hindus*, SCM Press, 1996.

[2] D. Bonhoeffer, *Letters and Papers from Prison*, SCM Press 1953, p. 163. Van Buren begins his book *The Secular Meaning of the Gospel*, SCM Press 1963, p. 1 with a quotation from Bonhoeffer.

[3] J. Robinson, *Honest to God*, SCM Press 1963, p. 23.

[4] R. Bultmann's article first appeared in 1941 but was not translated into English until 1953.

[5] J. Robinson, *Honest to God*, SCM Press 1963, p. 24.

[6] *Chandogya Upanishad*. 7.1.1-3 Quotation abbreviated.

[7] *Chandogya Upanishad*, 6.1.3.

[8] L. Wittgenstein, *Logico-philosophicus*, 1966, pp. 114ff.

[9] Galatians 2:20.

[10] W. James, *The Varieties of Religious Experience*, Longmans, Green and Co,

London, 16th impression 1908, p. 419.

11 The English translation from the Greek is by Murray Rogers in an article by Fr M. Rogers, 'My Gift from Hindu Friends' in *World Faiths*, No 99, Summer 1976, p. 20. I quote the poem in full in my *The Explorer's Guide to Christianity*, Hodder and Stoughton, 1998, pp. 250-251.

12 *The Fourth R for the Third Millennium: Education in Religion and Values for the Global Future*, Veritas Company (UK) Leamington 2001. Report in the *Church Times* 16.3.2001, p. 4.

THE PRAYER OF SILENCE

'Your true praise consists in perfect silence,' wrote the Hindu poet and teacher Dnyanadev (fl. 1290) in his commentary on the *Bhagavad Gita*. God, he said, does not put on any other ornament except silence.[1]

The Prayer of Silence, or Centring Prayer as it is sometimes called, has in recent years become quite well known in the West. When I first went to India, however, like many Western Christians, I was used to verbal worship and prayer addressed to a transcendent God. India helped me to discover the prayer of silence to the God within.

Fr Murray Rogers told me that he once took a Hindu friend to a church service. Afterwards, the Hindu friend said that he had appreciated the service, but added, 'Tell me, Murray, when do you pray?' There had been a series of readings and hymns and prayers, but not the silence that the Hindu friend had expected.

Speaking to God as to a friend through Jesus Christ is the pattern of prayer and worship in which I was brought up and which I continue to value. But with a close friend or a lover there can be times of companionable silence as well as of conversation. One rejoices to be in the other's presence. In Hinduism, as we shall see, rather than sharing in congregational worship, a person goes to a temple just to see the deity for what is called *darshan*. It is enough just to be in the presence of the Divine. There is an old story of a French peasant who used to spend long hours in church.

When asked what he did, he replied, 'I look at him [the image of Christ] and he looks at me.'

The prayer of silence and of waiting or being in the presence of God is very much part of the Christian contemplative and mystical tradition, which in recent years has become better known. It is perhaps worth noting the rather different use of the word meditation in East and West. In the West, meditation, as for example taught by Ignatius Loyola (1495-1556) who founded the Society of Jesus (Jesuits), although intended to lead from the head to the heart, was based on imaginative reading of scripture. It began with the use of the discursive intellect. Silent prayer, which in the East is called meditation but in the West is usually called contemplation, seeks to still the mind and to empty it of words and images.

There are various different schools of meditation - here I use the word in its Eastern meaning - but there are similarities. Most will teach the need for a balanced and comfortable physical posture, but not all Westerners can adapt to the traditional cross-legged yoga position. Stress is put on the breathing. Slow deep breathing helps to still the body and the mind. In some Buddhist schools, awareness of the breathing is sufficient. Other schools suggest the repetition of a sacred word or *mantra*. The purpose is not so much to think about the word but by its repetition to still the endless stream of thoughts. Members of the International Society for Krishna Consciousness repeatedly chant the words '*Hare Krishna, Hare Krishna, Krishna Krishna, Hare Hare, Hare Rama, Rama Rama, Hare Hare.*' Others, for example, the Brahma Kumaris, may encourage visualization of the pure soul at one with the Divine. Some people prefer to fix their gaze on a flower or an image of the divine whereas others meditate with the eyes closed.

The method is relatively unimportant; the hope is in the stillness to sense the presence of the Divine. Some meditation schools seem to suggest that such an experience is the result of following the practices they teach. Too easily meditation - and its accompanying spiritual experiences - can seem to be presented as development of innate human potential. This, I think, is misleading, as the sense of the presence of the Divine is always a gift of God not something that we can command or arrange to order - even though God longs for us to be aware of the Divine presence.

Anthony Bloom writes of an old lady who told him that although she had prayed continuously for fourteen years she had never sensed the presence of God. He gave her wise advice and later she told him of her first experience. She had gone into her room, made herself comfortable, and begun to knit. She felt relaxed and then she gradually became aware that the silence was not simply the absence of sound. 'All of a sudden,' she said, 'I perceived that the silence was a presence. At the heart of the silence there was Him.'[2]

I like Ann Lewin's comparison of waiting in prayer for God to watching for a kingfisher.

Prayer is like watching
for the kingfisher.
All you can do is
Be where he is likely to appear
And wait.
Often, nothing much happens:
There is space, silence
And expectancy.
No visible sign.
Only the Knowledge
That He's been there
And may come again.
Seeing or not seeing cease to matter,
You have been prepared.

But sometimes when you've almost
Stopped expecting it,
a flash of brightness
Gives encouragement.[3]

Father Keating, a teacher of Centring Prayer, says that we may well spend twenty minutes trying to quieten the mind, but it is time well spent if it leads to one minute of deep silence.

I have spoken of waiting to sense the presence of God. That, however, is not the hope of all who meditate. Buddhists, at least of the Theravadin tradition, do not speak of God. For them, meditation is a way of learning to live fully in the present and to develop total awareness. I once spent a day in Buddhist meditation in which we alternated between sitting and concentrating on our breathing and the walking meditation in which we learned to focus fully on the act of walking - feeling the movement of the muscles and the pressure of the foot on the ground. Full concentration on the present is of great value. Too often we are thinking about something that has occurred or may be going to happen and are not fully focused on what we are actually doing.

For the theist, however, learning to be still is a preparation for the meeting with God for which a devotee yearns. 'I live in the hope of meeting him,' writes Rabindranath Tagore in *Gitanjali*, 'I have not seen his face, nor have I listened to his voice; only I have heard his gentle footsteps from the road before my house.'[4] Later, Tagore writes:

Have you not heard his silent steps?
He comes, comes, ever comes.
Every moment and every age,
every day and every night
he comes, comes, ever comes.
Many a song have I sung in many a mood of mind,

but all their notes have always proclaimed,
'He comes, comes, ever comes.'[5]

Not all Hindus think of the Real in theistic terms. According to the teaching of Advaita, in meditation one becomes aware of the ultimate oneness of the self with the Self of all that is - *atman* is *Brahman*. Many Westerners, I think, misrepresent the subtlety of Advaita Vedanta and describe it as Monism or pantheism. Sankara (c. 788-820), the great teacher of Advaita, speaks of the world as *Maya*. The word is sometimes translated as 'illusion', but that may be misleading. The key to Sankara's thinking, explains T. M. P. Mahadevan, a distinguished philosopher who was himself an Advaitin, is that 'he postulates two standpoints: the absolute and the relative. The supreme truth is that *Brahman* is non-dual and relationless. It alone is; there is nothing real besides it. But from our standpoint, which is the empirical, relative standpoint, *Brahman* appears as God, the cause of the world.'[6] Just as we might mistake a coiled rope for a snake, so from our standpoint we think the world is real. If, however, we attain realization or *moksa*, then, from that standpoint we see the unreality of the empirical world. The Vedas teach this according to Sankara, although he insists that we need to realize this truth in experience and *jnana yoga*, which includes meditation, is the way to that experience.

Some Christians, such as Fr Bede Griffiths, related Christian experience closely to that of Advaita Vedanta. I have myself always felt closer to theistic Hinduism and the teachings of Ramanuja (eleventh or twelfth century), who founded the school of philosophy known as Visistadvaita or qualified non-dualism. Ramanuja held that individual selves and the world of matter are real, but that they are always dependent on Brahman for their existence and functions. We shall refer to these two strands in Hindu philosophy again in the next chapter.

Let me here pursue some of the consequences of learning the prayer of silence for my understanding of God. One is the awareness, which as we have seen is at the heart of Hindu teaching, that the reality of the Divine cannot be fully described in words. God is more wonderful than any words that we use. This implies that what we say or write about the Ultimate Mystery is bound to be tentative, which makes me hesitant about bold affirmations of faith or too literal a reading of scripture. It has also meant that in preaching, I have tried to avoid telling people what to believe and tried to encourage them to explore their own spiritual experience.

Silent prayer has also deepened my awareness of God's immanence or presence in my inner being. Many traditional Christian images echo Isaiah's vision of 'the Lord seated on a throne, high and exalted.'[7] Even Jesus has been pictured as a great king, more splendid that any emperor, sitting in judgement on the world. Such a God is bound to appear distant and remote. Yet, as in the silence we fathom the depths of our being, we become aware of the divine presence within. For me, it not the oneness of Advaita but the fullest possible communion of love.

Breathe on me, Breath of God;
Till I am wholly thine,
Until this earthly part of me
Glows with thy fire divine.[9]

The mystical and the charismatic, although very different in their outer manifestations, have a similar emphasis on experience of the Spirit of God. Hinduism helped me to turn with appreciation to the mystical tradition in Christianity and to discover the reality of the Spirit's presence in the heart.

But is it one and the same Divine Spirit who comes to Hindu

and Christian alike? With the World Congress of Faiths I helped to arrange a series of Meditation Weekends, which Bishop George Appleton or I led jointly with Swami Bhavyananda of the Ramakrishna Vedanata Movement. Each of us led times of meditation according to our own tradition and I think all present found that the teaching of both traditions led them closer to the Ultimate Divine Reality. But do all religions really lead to the same goal?

---

[1] Quoted in *The Gift of Prayer*, ed. J. T. Kieling, SCM Press, 1995, No 94, p. 56.

[2] A. Bloom, *School for Prayer*, Darton, Longman and Todd, 1970, pp. 60f.

[3] A. Lewin in *Laughter, Silence and Shouting*, ed. K. Keay, HarperCollins, 1994, p. 172.

[4] R. Tagore, *Gitanjali*, 1912, Papermac edition, Macmillan, 1986, 13, p. 11.

[5] R. Tagore, *Gitanjali*, 1912, Papermac edition, Macmillan, 1986, 45, pp. 36-37.

[6] T. M. P. Mahadevan, *Outlines of Hinduism*, Chetana, Bombay, 1956, p. 145.

[7] Isaiah 6:1.

[8] From the hymn by Edwin Hatch (1835-89).

DO ALL RELIGIONS LEAD TO GOD?

'We accept all religions as true,' Swami Vivekananda told members of the World Parliament of Religions, which was held in Chicago in 1893.[1] In this he was echoing the teaching of his guru Sri Ramakrishna.

As a student, the young Narenda, as Vivekananda was then known, asked several of his teachers at the Scottish Church College in Calcutta, 'Sir, have you seen God?' One of the teachers told him of a Hindu seer called Sri Ramakrishna, who might be able to answer 'yes' to his question. The extraordinary experiences of his first meetings with Sri Ramakrishna quickly convinced Narenda that here was someone with direct experience of the Divine rather than intellectual knowledge about God. In time, Vivekananda was to make Sri Ramakrishna known to the world.[2]

Sri Ramakrishna (1836-86) was born in a village in Bengal. At the age of nineteen he became a priest at the Kali temple at Dakshineswar, near Calcutta, where the Sri Ramakrishna Mission has built a beautiful temple, which I once visited after an endless drive through the crowded streets of Calcutta. Ramakrishna, after a time of intense devotion, eventually realized the presence of the goddess Kali. His biographer wrote, 'While he sat down to worship, a curtain of oblivion separated him from the outside world ... While uttering the various *mantras* (or sacred verses) he could distinctly see those phenomena before him which the ordinary priest has merely to imagine.'[3] Ramakrishna then focused his attention on the god Rama.[4] He put himself in the place of Hanuman, the monkey god who was a devotee of Rama and began to imitate his actions. In due course he had a vision of Sita, Rama's consort, and of the child Rama.

Following other spiritual disciplines, Ramakrishna had visions of the god Krishna, the Eternal Lover. Later in life, he was instructed in Advaita Vedanta and we are told that on the very first day he attained the mystical experience of unity, which is the culmination of that discipline. After a time, he followed the devotional path of the Sufis or Muslim mystics and had a vision of the Prophet Muhammad. Ramakrishna, who had some knowledge of the Bible, then turned to Christianity and received a vision of Jesus.

Ramakrishna insisted that it was the One Divine Reality whom he had experienced in his various visions. The unity of religion was for him not a matter of argument but of experience. In a tribute to Sri Ramakrishna, the poet Rabindranath Tagore wrote,

> Diverse courses of worship
> from varied springs of fulfillment
> have mingled in your meditation.
> The manifold revelation of joy of the Infinite
> has given form to a shrine of unity
> in your life.[5]

Some three hundred years before Guru Nanak (1469-1539), the founder of the Sikh religion, made a similar claim. He declared that he would follow God's path and that 'God's path was neither Hindu nor Muslim.'[6] Kabir (d. 1518), the mystic and religious reformer, said the same,

> Says Kabir at the top of his voice:
> There is but One and the Same God,

Both for Hindus and Muslims.[7]

Ramakrishna's claims have occasioned wide discussion about the nature of mystical experience. They also provided a basis on which modern Hindus could resist the call to them of missionaries to convert to Christianity. Further, the testimony of Ramakrishna and other mystics may suggest that human beings are naturally religious and this, as I have already indicated, has influenced my attempt to relate Christian faith to moments of heightened awareness, which are more common than is usually recognized. Sri Ramakrishna has had a profound influence on my thinking and writing.

Is all mystical experience essentially the same?

Ramakrishna's claim was that spiritual experience is one and that religious differences are caused by cultural and historical variations. This view has been adopted by a number of writers on Mysticism. Paul Elmer More, for example, wrote in his *Christian Mysticism*, which was published in 1932:

> There is a ground of psychological experience, potential in all men, actually realized in a few, common to all mystics of all lands and times and accountable for the similarity of their reports. But upon that common basis we need not be surprised to see them also erecting various superstructures in accordance with their particular tenets of philosophy or religion. At bottom, their actual experiences, at the highest point at least, will be amazingly alike, but their theories in regard to what happened to them may be radically different.[8]

Walter Stace, in his *The Teachings of the Mystics*, made the same claim: 'The same mystical experience may be interpreted by a Christian in terms of Christian beliefs and by a Buddhist in terms of Buddhist beliefs.'[9] The Indian philosopher Sarvepalli Radhakrishnan also said, 'The seers describe their experiences with an impressive unanimity. They are near to one another on mountains farthest apart.'[10]

This view, however, has been disputed. R. C. Zaehner, who was Spalding Professor of Eastern Religions and Ethics at Oxford, argued, in his *Mysticism, Sacred and Profane*, that there are different types of mystical experience. Zaehner distinguished three main categories. The first is 'nature mysticism', wherein the mystic is sensibly aware of the natural world, but feels no distinction between himself and the natural world. Wordsworth in some of his poems speaks of 'the calm that Nature breathes among the hills and groves.'[11] 'I felt,' he wrote, 'the sentiment of Being spread o'er all that moves and all that seemeth still.'[12] Zaehner's second category is what is called a 'monistic experience' where a person feels a total oneness with the Soul of the Universe. An example of this is the Hindu seer Sri Ramana Maharshi (1879-1950), who has been called, paradoxically, 'an incarnation of pure Advaita.'[13] As a teenager Ramana Maharshi dramatized his own death and thereby realized that the self is untouched by death and that it is one with the Self. Thirdly, there is theistic mystical experience in which 'the soul feels itself to be united with God in love.'[15] The word communion, which may be applied to this experience, suggests that the soul and God are distinct entities, however close their relationship. St Teresa of Avila (1515-82) spoke of union with God as 'spiritual marriage.'[15]

In his commentary on the *Bhagavad Gita*, Zaehner argued that the whole purpose of the text was 'to demonstrate that love of a personal God, so far from being *only* a convenient preparation for the grand unitary experience ... was also the crown of this experience itself, which, without it, must remain imperfect.'[16]

My own feeling, as I have suggested elsewhere, is that there are differences of mystical experience but, unlike Zaehner, I hesitate to assert that the theistic experience is higher than the monistic experience.[17]

An answer to Christian missions

If varieties of belief and practice are caused by cultural and historical differences and all religions are essentially the same, what is the point of trying to persuade people to change their religion? The nineteenth century was the great age of Christian mission - especially by Protestant churches - in Asia and Africa. Christian triumphalism, with its claim to the unique and final revelation of God, was evident also amongst many participants at the 1893 World Parliament of Religions in Chicago. Swami Vivekananda, however, provided an effective answer by basing his remarks on the experience and teaching of Sri Ramakrishna. Vivekananda argued that the same God is the inspirer of all religions. Appealing to the idea of evolution, which was much in people's minds at the time, he spoke of the knowledge and idea of God evolving in each religion. 'All religions from the lowest fetishism to the highest absolutism' are, he said, so many attempts of the human soul to grasp and realize the Infinite 'as determined by the condition of birth and association.' He quoted words of Krishna from the *Bhagavad Gita* that 'I am in every religion as the thread through a string of pearls.'[18]

In place of aggressive Christian evangelism, Vivekananda seized the moral high ground by implying that the missionaries' call for conversions was irrelevant and narrow-minded. Instead Vivekananda appealed for universal tolerance. In his reply to the welcome, part of which was quoted at the beginning of this chapter, he declared, 'I am proud to belong to a religion which has taught the world both tolerance and universal acceptance. We believe not only in universal toleration, but we accept all religions as true. I am proud to belong to a nation which has sheltered the persecuted and the refugees of all religions and all nations of the earth.'[19]

The importance of mutual respect between members of different religions is now widely recognized and the Christian denunciation of Hinduism as idolatrous, superstitious and polytheistic, which was common in the nineteenth century, is much rarer today. Yet the relation of religions to each other is still a subject of vigorous debate. At least at the level of their teachings and practices there are significant differences between religions. For example, some religions claim that human beings have only one life on earth, others suggest that the soul comes back again and again in different bodies. There is sharp disagreement on whether God has a Son. Religious rituals are very varied. Is there a common or unifying spiritual experience? Can we indeed speak of universal human experiences?

My own view is that there is one God who made and loves all people and seeks from them an answering love and obedience. The great religions of the world are channels of that divine love and human responses to it. Because they are human responses all are flawed. I do not think religions are all the same. Rather they are shaped by a creative experience of the Divine and by centuries of tradition and reflection. Each religion, as the American Catholic R. E. Whitson put it, is therefore 'unique and universal: unique in that the core of each is a distinct central experience - not to be found elsewhere - and universal in that this core experience is of supreme significance for all men.'[20] Each religion has a particular message or 'gospel' for the whole world. As we learn from each other, our understanding of the Divine Mystery will grow. There are in my view more and less adequate pictures of God and understandings of the divine purpose. For example, traditional Christian teaching about hell - especially as a punishment for non-believers who never heard of Jesus - cannot be squared with belief in a God who loves all human beings.

Three quotations from Fr Bede Griffiths put very well the

position I seek to advocate.

> This one Truth, which cannot be expressed, is present in all religion, making itself known, communicating itself by signs. The myths and rituals of primitive (*sic*) religion, the doctrines and sacraments of the more advanced (*sic*) are all signs of this eternal Truth, reflected in the consciousness of man. Each religion manifests some aspect of this one Reality, creates a system of symbols by which this Truth may be known, this reality experienced.[21]

> The Buddha, Krishna, Christ - each is a unique revelation of God, of the divine Mystery, and each has to be understood in its historical context, in its own peculiar mode of thought ... each revelation is therefore complementary to the other, and indeed in each religion we find a tendency to stress first one aspect of the Godhead and then another, always seeking that equilibrium in which the ultimate truth will be found.[22]

> The divine Mystery, the eternal Truth, has been revealing itself to all men from the beginning of history. Every people has received some insight into this divine Mystery - which is the mystery of human existence - and every religion ... has its own unique insight into the one Truth. These insights, insofar as they reflect the one Reality, are in principle complementary. Each has its own defects both of faith and practice, and each has to learn from others, so they may grow together to that unity in Truth which is the goal of human existence.[23]

Vivekananda's views are a particularly sharp challenge to Christians who believe that Jesus is the unique and only Son of God and Saviour of the world. Is it essential to believe in the Lord Jesus for a person to go to heaven? In part this depends on how

Christians understand the work of Christ, often known as the Atonement. A traditional belief is that Jesus Christ died on the cross for the sins of the whole world. If that is thought of as an objective event, which altered humanity's standing in relation to God, then the belief itself implies that it is significant for all people. Some Christians hold to this view but believe that the death of Jesus can be effective for people who lead good lives, even though they do not know of Jesus - people who are sometimes referred to as 'anonymous Christians'. An alternative understanding of the meaning of the death of Jesus is to think of it in a more personal and subjective way. By his willingness to die on the cross, Jesus showed that there is no limit to God's love for us. To believe this is to experience an inner change that frees us from our fears and by deepening our compassion makes us sorry for the lack of love and the selfishness in our lives. In gratitude we offer ourselves in loving service to the Lord.

The story of Jesus' death on the cross is the place where I have known most vividly the unlimited love and forgiveness of God, which has helped to free me from self-doubt and fear and enabled me to grow in love for others. I am glad to witness to this divine mercy and long for others to experience such forgiveness and peace for themselves. It is not, however, for me to pass judgement on the spiritual journey of others.

The hymns of the Tamil saints, for example, are rich in their testimony to the love and forgiveness of God. Manikavacakar (eighth or ninth century), for example, wrote,

When You, the Lord with an eye on the forehead,
arrived where I was,
and beckoned me with Your gracious glance, I of evil karma
did not in the least know
how to worship ...
O Reality! Your golden feet I saw this day

and deliverance from birth gained.[24]

or again

You bestowed on me a grace undeserved by me
and enabled this slave's body and soul
to joyfully thaw and melt with love.[25]

The Saivite saint, Tirunavukkarasar, (seventh century) said to God, 'I know you are merciful.'[26]

The inter-faith sharing for which I long, of which there is still too little, is to speak to each other of our experience of the grace of God - 'telling one another our beautiful names for God.' As the blind man in St John's gospel says, 'One thing I know, that whereas I was blind now I see.'[27] If others can say the same, let us rejoice together and learn from each other's story.

We should learn to see members of other faiths as fellow pilgrims. There are all too many people in our world who have little awareness of spiritual realities and religious communities have a responsibility to make known their teachings. I dislike, however, religious recruiting, although equally people should be free to change their religion if they feel this will help their spiritual growth. Donald Nichol in his book *Holiness*, [28] said that a sign of a faith community's maturity is the way in which it treats those who leave it. By that standard most faith communities are fairly immature. Those who change their religion or who wish to marry a member of another faith often experience strong opposition and rejection. There are many ways to God and each person should be encouraged to find the path which is most helpful to them, although they may need to be warned that others have found some paths to be dangerous or dead-ends. Perhaps we need to concentrate on making as much progress as possible on our chosen route rather than on criticizing the paths others are following. Certainly when St Peter asked Jesus what would happen to St John, he got short shrift. 'What is that to you? You must follow me.'[29]

Are human beings naturally religious?

Paul Elmer More, in a passage already quoted, suggested that the ground of psychological experience which finds its fullest expression in mysticism is potentially present in all people. He thereby challenged a widespread assumption, derived from the work of Sigmund Freud (1856-1938), the founder of psychoanalysis, that religion was a collective expression of neurosis and an attempt on the part of individuals to escape from the realities of a hostile and indifferent world. Karl Marx (1818-83), the founder of Communism, in a famous phrase, had also described religion as 'the opium of the people.'[30]

More's view has been supported by the work of Alister Hardy and the Religious Experience Research Centre. Alister Hardy sought to show that the human being is naturally religious. Alister Hardy, who was a marine biologist, built up an extensive archive of people's first-hand accounts of religious transcendental experience. He argued from this that a 'sense of Presence' was far more common than was usually recognized.

This is why, in my preaching and ministry, as I have said, I have tried to relate the Christian faith to people's sometimes inarticulate awareness of Divine reality, encouraging them to reflect on 'moments of mystery'. In this I am aware of following the example of the great theologian and preacher Freidrich Schleiermacher (1768-1834), who has been called the father of modern Protestant theology. Addressing the cultured despisers of religion of his generation, he urged them not to concentrate on doctrinal statements, which they mocked, but on a 'sense and taste for the Infinite' or, in a phrase that he often used, on 'a feeling of absolute dependence.' Religion, Schleiermacher said, 'is the immediate consciousness of the universal existence of all finite things in and through the Infinite, and of all temporal things in and through the Eternal.'[31]

Sri Ramakrishna's spiritual discoveries can still serve to encourage us to value our own, and other people's, moments of heightened awareness. He can inspire us to hope that despite the enormous variety of religious belief and practice, we can discover our oneness in the presence of God. Long ago, a Sufi poet Ibn Arabi (1165-1240) said, 'On my way to the mosque, O Lord, I passed the Magian in front of his flame, deep in thought, and a little further I heard a rabbi reciting his holy book in the synagogue, and then I came upon the church where the hymns sung gently in my ears and finally I came into the mosque and pondered how many are the different ways to You - the one God.'[32] More recently, the English writer on mysticism, Evelyn Underhill, said that religions meet where religions take their source - in God. Ramakrishna suggests, from his own experience, that all devotees, however they call upon God, are met by one and the same Divine Reality.

If, then, there are many ways to the One God, is it only in Jesus that God is fully revealed and does the Bible have an authority greater than that of other scriptures? These are questions to which we shall be returning chapters 5 and 6.

---

[1] *The World's Parliament of Religions*, ed. J. H. Barrows, The Parliament Publishing Co, Chicago, 1893, p. 977.

[2] S. Saradananda, *Shri Ramakrishan the Great Master*, 3rd edition p. 717 and pp. 736-7.

[3] Quoted by T. M. P. Mahadevan, *Outlines of Hinduism*, Chetana, Bombay, 1956, p. 217.

[4] See below, p. 59.

[5] Quoted by H. W. French, *The Swan's Wide Waters: Ramakrishna and Western Culture*, Kennikat Press, Port Washington, N.Y. 1974, p. 31.

[6] Quoted by M. P. Fisher, *Living Religions*, Prentice Hall, 4th edition 1999, p. 401.

[7] Quoted in H. Singh, *The Message of Sikhism*, Gurdwara Parbandahak Committee, Delhi, 1968.

[8] P. E. More, *Christian Mysticism*, SPCK, 1932, p. 93.

[9] W. Stace, *The Teachings of the Mystics*, New American Library, New York, 1960, p.12.

[10] S. Radhakrishnan, 'Fragments of a Confession' in *The Philosophy of Sarvepalli Radhakrishnan*, ed. A. Schlipp, Open Court, New York, 1952, p. 62.

[11] W. Wordsworth, *The Prelude*, I, 280-1.

[12] W. Wordsworth, *The Prelude*, II, 401-2.

[13] T. M. P. Mahadevan, *Outlines of Hinduism*, Chetana, Bombay, 1956.

[14] R. C. Zaehner, *Mysticism, Sacred and Profane*, Oxford University Press (1957), 1961 edition, p. 28.

[15] See the entry on Teresa of Avila in *The Oxford Dictionary of World Religions*, ed J. Bowker, p. 965.

[16] R. C. Zaehner, *The Bhagavad Gita*, Oxford, 1969, p. 3.

[17] See further my *Spiritual Experience That Crosses Religious Divisions*, 2nd series Occasional Paper 20, published by the Religious Experience Research Center, Oxford 1999, *passim*.

[18] *The World's Parliament of Religions*, ed. J. H. Barrows, The Parliament Publishing Co, Chicago, 1893, pp. 976-7. In the Gita, Krishna also says he regards even the humblest offering as a gift of love; 'Be it leaf or flower or fruit that a zealous soul may offer Me with love's devotion, that do I (willingly) accept, for it was love that made the offering.' (9, 26)

[19] *The World's Parliament of Religions*, ed. J. H. Barrows, The Parliament Publishing Co, Chicago, 1893, p. 102.

[20] R. E. Whitson, *The Coming Convergence of the World Religions*, Columbia University Press, 1963, p. 97.

[21] Quoted by J. B. Trapnell, *Bede Griffiths: A Life in Dialogue*, State University of New York Press, 2001, p. 150.

[22] B. Griffiths, *Return to the Centre*, Collins, 1976, pp. 86-7.

[23] B. Griffiths, *Vedanta and Christian Faith*, Dawn Horse Press, California, 1973, pp.7-8.

[24] Quoted in the *Lotus Prayer Book*, complied by Satchidananda ashram – Yogaville, 1986, p. 19.

[25] Quoted in the *Lotus Prayer Book*, complied by Satchidananda ashram – Yogaville, 1986, p. 101.

[26] Quoted in the *Lotus Prayer Book*, complied by Satchidananda ashram – Yogaville, 1986, p. 103. See also R. Otto, *India's Religions of Grace and Christianity*, 1930.

[27] John 9:25.

[28] D. Nicholl, *Holiness*, Darton, Longman and Tudd,1981

[29] John 21:22.

[30] K. Marx, *A Contribution to the Critique of Hegel's Philosophy of Right*, 1843-4, Introduction.

[31] See further my *The Explorer's Guide to Christianity*, Hodder and Stoughton, 1998, pp 10-14.

[32] Ibn Arabi in *Tarjuman al-Ashwaq*.

IMAGES OF GOD

I have come to appreciate the beauty of many Hindu temples, but my first visit to a big temple in Madras was bewildering. I vividly recall the heat, especially of the sandy earth on which one had to walk barefoot, the various smells, the dirt, and above all the number and variety of images of God.[1]

Hindu images of the Divine have provoked a strong and negative reaction in many Western visitors. Diana Eck, writing of the holy city of Varanasi (formerly known as Banaras), says it was the multitude of divine images

> more than anything else, that elicited the strongest response of Westerners in their encounter with Banaras and with Hinduism generally. Virtually everyone who visited the city, from Ralph Fitch in the sixteenth century through those who went there in subsequent centuries, expressed astonishment and even repugnance at the panoply of images. Fitch wrote 'Their chief idols (*sic*) bee blacke and evil-favoured, their mouth monstrous, their ears gilded and full of jewels, their teeth and eyes of gold, silver, and glasse, some having one thing in their handes and some another.' Three hundred years later, the English assessment of these images had changed little. In the 1800s, Norman Macleod, in the midst of his exuberance for the vistas of Banaras, referred to 'that ugly looking monster called God,' and M. A. Sherring wrote of 'the worship of uncouth images, of monsters, of the *linga* and other indecent figures, and of a

multitude of grotesque, ill-shapen, and hideous objects.'[2]

The missionary Henry Martyn spoke of a visit to a Hindu temple as like being in the vicinity of hell.

In some of the Western reaction there is an aesthetic as well as a religious antipathy. The sculpture of Ancient Greece, often of Olympian deities, was admired but the exuberance of much Hindu art was puzzling and Pöhlmann writes that 'what is annoying about many images of the gods is their kitsch,' although he adds that kitsch is a very relative term.[3] Westerners too, reared on the Bible with its denunciations of 'idolatry', felt little sympathy with Hindu devotion and some would refuse the gift of *prasad,* a sweet, which after being offered to the god is given to the devotee. I remember that some Christians at Madras Christian College were shocked that I should want to visit a Hindu temple.

The mistake, however, is to assume that the image is in fact the object of worship rather than a representation of the Divine who is formless. The book of Isaiah misses the point with its mockery:

> Half of the wood he burns in the fire; over it he prepares his meal, he roasts his meat and eats his fill. He also warms himself and says, 'Ah, I am warm; I see the fire.' From the rest he makes a god, his image; he bows down to it and worships. He prays to it and says, 'Save me; you are my god.' They know nothing, they understand nothing.[4]

The Book of Wisdom is rather more sympathetic. 'Small blame,' it says, 'attaches to those who go astray in their search for God and eagerness to find him and fall victim to appearances, seeing so much beauty.'[5]

Hindu teachers make clear that the ultimate divine reality, *Brahman*, is beyond all forms and description, but such a Deity is too remote for many people. God, therefore, graciously makes himself available to worshippers in the form of an image. In the Gita (4,11), Krishna tells Arjuna 'In whatever way people approach me, in that way do I show them favour.' The great Hindu teacher Ramanuja (eleventh century), who in his commentary says that the Lord is characterized by his utter supremacy and his gracious accessibility, explains that this verse means 'in that way do I make myself visible to them.'[6] The Lord becomes accessible both in images and in incarnations. It is, as another Vaisnavite theologian, Pillai Lokacarya, explained, one more evidence of God's graciousness. 'This is the greatest grace of the Lord,' he wrote, 'that being free he becomes bound, being independent he becomes dependent for all His service on His devotee ... The Infinite has become finite that the child soul may grasp, understand and love Him.'[7]

The image brings God into focus - it is not in itself a god. Yet after the ceremony of consecration, as Fr Fallon points out, 'the devout worshipper believes that something has happened, the statue or image has been transformed into the very body of god or at least, into his abode.'[8] As Diana Eck explains, 'Because the image is a form of the Supreme Lord, it is precisely the image that facilitates and enhances the close relationship of the worshipper and God and makes possible the deepest outpourings of emotions in worship.'[9] In the temple ritual, whereby, like a royal personage, the image is woken in the morning, honoured with song and incense, dressed and fed, the worshipper expresses his or her devotion to God. There are perhaps parallels with the devotion shown by some Christians to the consecrated bread and wine at the Mass. For myself, I think of Christ's presence in the fellowship of believers who remember him rather than localized in the host, but as Fr Fallon says, 'The "sacramentalism" which characterizes true Christianity should help us see what there is of positive value in the "symbolism" of the Hindu religious world.'[10] A sympathetic attempt to understand the value of images for Hindus has also helped me to appreciate the value of icons for Orthodox Christians and the many statues of Mediterranean or Latin American Catholic churches.

Images that help some people, get in the way for others. Several Hindu reformers from Kabir to Tagore, as well as Sikh gurus and Indian Muslims, have condemned images. Others see their value as only for the spiritually uneducated. Lokacarya, as we have seen, spoke of the child soul. The orthodox writer Raghunanda said the same: 'For the sake of the devotee do we fancy forms and shapes of that Brahman, which is pure spirit, the one without a second, the absolutely simple and incorporeal One.'[11] Some twentieth-century Hindu leaders, such as Vivekananda and Dr Radhakrishnan, have taken the same view. It is sometimes said that in all religions people need a material focus for their devotion. One devotee of the god Rama explained, 'God without form is too remote, you cannot reach him, therefore all men worship him in some form that brings him near. Muslims have the Qur'an, Sikhs the Guru Granth Sahib, and Christians the Cross.'[12] Dr C. T. K. Chari, my professor of philosophy at Madras Christian College, never went to a temple. He considered it unnecessary for the spiritually educated and he explained that the images in his home were for the benefit of his wife and children!

My own preference is for simplicity, but Hinduism has helped me to see the value of colour and movement in worship and to be more appreciative of those whose devotion is expressed through arranging the flowers, polishing the brasses and ensuring that the church communicates 'the beauty of holiness'.

The Hindu devotee approaches the god of the temple or indeed a guru for *darshan* or a viewing of the divine. Hindu worship, which is individual and not congregational, is not primarily a matter of prayers and offerings. It is eye contact with the divine image that brings blessing, power, comfort and forgiveness, as is true of Benediction, a Catholic eucharistic devotion wherein the consecrated host is exposed to view in a monstrance. The Hindu devotee longs to stand in the presence of the image and to see and be seen by the deity. There is a great sense of excitement in the temple as the curtains are drawn back and the image is revealed to the view of the worshippers. Gifts are taken not to atone for sins or to win favours but to express delight in God, just as when one visits a friend one does not go empty handed.[13] Again, this desire to see and to be in the presence of the divine is a reminder also that worship is not just a matter of belief but of presence - of sensing a mystery and beauty and peace that passes all understanding.

India, as Diana Eck observes, is a visual and visionary culture. What is seen, because of what it represents, is more important than what is heard. As Swami Kriyananda says, 'Words are but symbols. They do not present.'[14] Protestant Christianity, by contrast, with its emphasis on the Bible as the Word, has given primary importance to hearing and to reading. With the prevalence of television and computers, Western society has become more visual. Christian worship would perhaps be enriched by more colour. At a deeper level, there is the need to recover an awareness of the importance of symbols. The analytic and scientific approach to education has its limitations. The deepest truths can only be expressed in poetry, myth and symbol as some of the most successful authors of children's stories have realized. We need to be in touch with both the female or imaginative left side of the brain as well as the male analytical right side of the brain. As Bede Griffiths wrote, 'Man cannot live without myth; reason cannot live without the imagination ... The myth has to be reborn.'[15]

If some Westerners find the images of gods off-putting, they may also express surprise at finding that the *lingam*, the male organ, is the focus of worship in many temples dedicated to Siva, the third god of the Hindu trinity. The *lingam* is usually set in the *yoni,* a representation of the female vulva. In 1962 a respected scholar Gopinath Kaviraja explained that worship of the *lingam* was very ancient and purity and impurity are in the eye of the beholder. Creation, he said, always proceeds by the union of two powers, which are called by various names. This duality derives from the single ultimate source of all being.[16] The union of the *lingam* and *yoni* is the expression of creative energy.

Hindu gods are also usually shown with a consort. Indeed archaeological evidence suggests that reverence for the female as the source of life was of primary importance in the earliest Indian cultures. The Mother figure vividly expresses God's love for human beings. The worship of Sakti, divine female power, addressed also as Kali, Durga, Radha, Sarasvati, Laksmi, Ganga and Parvati, is still widespread, although often during periods of male domination, the goddess was brought into a relationship with a god, so that her powers were seen as an extension of his power.

A female deity was a surprise to me when I first went to India and brought to mind Old Testament denunciations of Baal worship and flagrant sexuality. Stories of temple prostitutes lurked somewhere at the back of my mind. Yet the language we use of God is only analogous. God is not literally a Father and there is no reason not to picture God as a mother or to call on 'God, our Parent.' Where possible, I now try to avoid the use of the male pronoun for God and I am disappointed that the churches are so slow to use inclusive language for God. We may now speak of 'humankind' but the language of 'Father, Son and Holy Spirit' is unchanged and the Holy Spirit, if given a gender is, like the worshipper, assumed to be male.[17] The accusation that the Church by the masculine nature of the language it has used of God has for centuries reflected and reinforced a patriarchal society, which has shut out female forms of self-representation and seen women in terms of male desire, is hard to refute.[18]

Women in India too have been the victims of male oppression, but whereas in much of Christianity there has been a fear of human sexuality, in some forms of theistic Hinduism sexuality and divine energy are related. This too may lead to abuse, but as Pöhlmann comments, 'In contrast to the devaluation of the body in the history of Christianity, from the beginning Hinduism had a more open relationship to the body, to sexuality and beauty.'[19] He mentions in particular scenes of Krishna playing his flute for the milkmaids to dance to which are a common theme of Indian art. He also refers to Günther Grass who called Hinduism a 'sensual religion'. Maybe a more positive valuing of human sexuality, which is evident in contemporary Christian thought, may help to combat the trivializing of it in Western society.

Images of Kali can at first sight be off-putting. The challenge of Kali, however, is to recognize the terrifying aspect of divine creative energy. Nature is 'red in tooth and claw'. If God is the source of all that is, God's ultimate responsibility for evil has to be recognized unless one moves into a dualism, which posits an Evil Power in competition with God. There is in Isaiah the puzzling verse, 'I form the light, and create darkness: I make peace, and create evil: I the Lord do all these things.'[20]

My involvement in Christian-Jewish relations and therefore with the theological implications of the Holocaust have led me to ponder this question and what I learned of the Hindu trinity, who is Creator, Sustainer and Destroyer, has helped me to believe that God is both life-giver and destroyer, present in life and death, in joy and sorrow.[21] Certainly I do not think God sends evil as a punishment, although life's difficulties may be a challenge. God wills what is best for all people, but I do believe that in the midst of evil God is present and by sharing our suffering God can help to transform it. For it is my confidence that no power in life or in death is stronger than the self-giving love of God, revealed for me most clearly in Jesus Christ.

Perhaps these mysteries are best expressed in myth and images and not in words. Although some of the images of the divine in Hinduism may seem alien and disturbing, they may also help us fathom mysteries beyond our comprehension.

---

1 I choose the word 'image' as a neutral term. Idol or icon may both imply a value judgement.

2 D. Eck, *Banaras: City of Light*, RKP, 1983, pp. 18f.

3 H. G. Pöhlmann, *Encounters with Hinduism*, SCM Press, 1996, pp. 32-3.

4 Isaiah 44:16-18.

5 Wisdom 13:6-7.

6 Quoted by D. Eck, *Darsan: Seeing the Divine Image in India*, Anima Books, 1981, p. 35.

7 Quoted in B. Kumarappa, *The Hindu Conception of Deity as Culminating in Ramanuja*, Luzac and Co, 1934, pp. 316-7.

8 P. Fallon in *Religious Hinduism: A Presentation and Appraisal*, by Jesuit Scholars, St Paul's Publications, Allahabad, 1968, p. 174 but see the whole chapter.

9 D. Eck, *Darsan: Seeing the Divine Image in India*, Anima Books, 1981, p. 35.

10 D. Eck, *Darsan: Seeing the Divine Image in India*, Anima Books, 1981, p. 179.

11 Quoted by P. Fallon in *Religious Hinduism: A Presentation and Appraisal*, by Jesuit Scholars, St Paul's Publications, Allahabad, 1968, p. 75.

12 Quoted by R. Hooker, *What is Idolatry*, British Council of Churches, 1986, p. 12.

13 See further H. G. Pöhlmann, *Encounters with Hinduism*, pp. 24-34.

14 S. Krityananda, *The Hindu Way of Awakening: Its Revelation, Its Symbols*, Cristal Clarity Publishers, Nevada City, CA, 1998, p. 19.

15 B. Griffiths, *The Marriage of East and West*, Collins and Templegate Publishers, Illinois, 1982, pp. 171 and 198-9. See also *Return to the Centre*,

Collins and Templegate Publishers, Illinois, 1976.

16 See further R. Hooker, *What is Idolatry*, British Council of Churches, 1986, pp. 18-19.

17 See the final lines of that beautiful hymn

'Come down O Love Divine':
Till *he* become the place
Wherein the Holy Spirit makes *his* dwelling.

18 See, for example, the writings of L. Irigaray, 'Equal to Whom?' in *The Post-Modern God*, ed. G. Ward, Blackwell, Oxford, 1997.

19 H. G. Pöhlmann, *Encounters with Hinduism*, SCM Press, 1996, p. 4.

20 Isaiah 45:7. This is the *Authorized Version* text. Modern translations somewhat soften the translation.

21 See *Dialogue With A Difference*, ed. T. Bayfield and M. Braybrooke, SCM Press, 1992, chapter 7.

Jesus

When I first visited Gobind Sadan, a Sikh inter-faith community on the outskirts of New Delhi, some eighteen years ago, the receptionist told me how she prayed every day that she would have a vision of Jesus. When we went back in 2001, the same woman shared with our group the vision she had had quite recently of Jesus, as a luminous figure standing beside her, who assured her of his love and blessing. The woman remains a devout Sikh.

The founder and leader of the ashram, HH Baba Virsa Singh himself had a vision of Jesus some years ago - and he told us of a recent vision of the Prophet Muhammad. As a result of his vision of Jesus, Baba Virsa Singh created a beautiful garden, known as the Jesus place, which has in it a statue of Jesus.

On our recent visit, we arrived just in time for the evening prayers at the Jesus place, during which hundreds of candles are lit and placed before the statue. We noticed that Jesus was wearing a coat and a woollen hat. Because nights in February are chilly, every evening a Sikh comes and puts them on the statue. The Jesus place is a favourite spot for members of the ashram and visitors to come and pray and we made our way back there several times.

Some Hindu holy men, especially, as we have seen, the influential nineteenth-century teacher Sri Ramakrishna, have also claimed to have had a vision of Jesus. Many other Hindus and Sikhs have a great love for Jesus. Indeed when my friend Professor Seshagiri Rao, a distinguished Hindu scholar, was asked to address an international Christian missionary conference, he began by saying, 'I speak to you as a fellow lover of Jesus Christ ...'

During the last two centuries a number of Indians have responded sympathetically to Jesus and tried to see his significance in an Indian context. Fr Hans Staffner, a Jesuit who was born in Austria but whose working life was spent in India, distinguishes three groups of Indian admirers of Jesus.[1]

Firstly, a number of Hindus admire Jesus as a moral teacher and example. The early nineteenth-century reformer Raja Ram Mohan Roy (1772-1833), who is buried at the Arnos Grove Cemetery at Bristol, wrote, 'I found the doctrine of Christ more conducive to inculcate moral principles and better adapted to rational beings than any other that has come to my knowledge.'[2] Mahatma Gandhi (1869-1948), who often spoke of Jesus, wrote 'the gentle figure of Christ, so patient, so kind, so loving, so full of forgiveness that he taught his followers not to retaliate when abused or struck but to turn the other cheek - it was a beautiful example, I thought, of the perfect man.'[3] Jesus, he said, 'was non-violence *par excellence*.'[4]

Staffner's second category is Hindus who were intensely committed to Jesus Christ but did not wish to join any existing Christian church. He takes as examples, Keshab Chandra Sen (1838-84) who for a time was leader of the Brahmo Samaj and who founded the Church of the New Dispensation and P. T. Mozoomdar (1840-1905), author of *The Oriental Christ*. Both had a deep love for Jesus but insisted he was an Asian not a European. 'The Western Christ,' Keshub Chandra Sen said, 'was not congenial to the Indian mind ... the picture of Christ's life and character is altogether a picture of ideal Hindu life.'[5] To this group might be added those Hindus who regard Jesus as an *avatar* or '*an* incarnation.'

Staffner's third category is Hindus who were baptized and became Christians but claimed that being Hindu by birth they remained socially and culturally Hindu. Staffner includes Brahmobandhav Upadhyaya (1861-1907), a close friend of Swami

Vivekananda, who tried to interpret Christianity in Indian philosophical categories, Narayan Vaman Tilak (1861-1919), who is loved throughout Maharashtra as 'the poet of children and flowers,' and Pandita Ramabai (1858-1922), who saw in Jesus Christ the hope and salvation of Indian womanhood. Those who belonged to Staffner's second and third categories wished to separate Jesus from the Western cultural dress and thought forms in which he was presented by missionaries.[6]

Although a number of Indian Christian thinkers have tried to interpret Jesus in Indian terms, my first impression of the Indian church in the sixties was that it was very Western and that many Indian Christians wished to maintain a distance from the surrounding Hindu society. I was, however, quickly made aware both of the deep love that many Indians have for Jesus and their difficulties with the exclusive Christian claim that Jesus is the unique Son of God. 'Let us find God not only in Jesus of Nazareth but in all the Great Ones that have preceded him and all that are yet to come' said Swami Vivekananda.[7] Mahatma Gandhi also said, 'I cannot ascribe exclusive divinity to Jesus. He is as divine as Krishna or Rama or Muhammad or Zoroaster.'[8]

RAMA AND KRISHNA

India has its own tradition of divine incarnations and this may make a special bond between Hinduism and Christianity.[9] The word *avatar* means literally a 'coming down' or 'manifestation'. One of the three high gods, Vishnu, is believed of his free choice on occasion to have taken bodily form as an animal or as a human being,

> For the protection of the virtuous,
> For the destruction of the wicked
> For the establishment of Right (*dharma*).[10]

The best-known incarnations are Rama and Krishna, in whom Vishnu took on a fully human life, including conception, birth and a natural death.

Rama

Rama, who perhaps most powerfully embodies the traditional Indian notions of *dharma* or righteousness, is the hero of the major epic called the *Ramayana*. This tells of his birth and childhood and his life in the sacred city of Ayodhya,[11] from which after a court intrigue he was banished to a forest. He was accompanied by his faithful wife Sita but she was abducted by Ravana, the demon king of Lanka. Eventually, with the help of his monkey friends and especially of the monkey god Hanuman, Rama defeated Ravana and rescued Sita. Rama, however, did not believe Sita's protestations that she had remained faithful to him whilst a prisoner of Ravana. Sita therefore had a funeral pyre built on which she threw herself but was rescued by the gods. Rama and Sita returned to Ayodhya, but because of false rumours that Sita had been unfaithful she was banished but eventually restored, although by that time her heart was broken. The epic ends with their death and ascent to heaven.

It is said that 'whoever reads and recites the holy, life-giving *Ramayana* is freed from sin and attains heaven.' The same result is achieved by anyone who, like Gandhi, repeats the name of Rama as he or she is dying or, for a dying person, by someone repeating the name of Rama in his or her ear.[12]

Krishna

In the vast literature about Krishna, he is seen as the divine child, the young herdsman and endearing lover and as an avatar of God. The stories of his childhood appeal to the maternal instinct and in many villages women worship the divine child. The young Krishna's love for the milk maidens is interpreted as symbolic of God's love for the human soul, which is called to respond to that divine love. In the *Bhagavad Gita* Krishna is seen as a personal God, the source of life and the sustainer of virtue.

The *Gita*, which is part of a massive epic poem called the *Mahabharata*, explores the crisis of conscience that faces the warrior Arjuna when he finds himself opposed in battle by members of his own family. The charioteer, Krishna in disguise, tells Arjuna that it is his duty as a warrior to fight, but Krishna's teaching goes far beyond this. Krishna says that only deeds, which are done without attachment to their results and through devotion (*bhakti*) to God and with trust in God's grace, can lead to realization of the Divine. Krishna indicates the three paths of knowledge, action with detachment and of love, which can lead to full knowledge of God. The climax of the *Gita* is Krishna's stupendous theophany when Arjuna is granted a 'celestial eye' (11, 8) whereby he can see the transfiguration of Krishna into the 'Self which does not pass away.' (11, 1-4). Arjuna, rather like Job, is overwhelmed with a sense of unworthiness and sin. Krishna comforts him and once again assumes 'the body of a friend' (11, 50).[13]

HISTORICITY

Parallels have been drawn between the stories of Jesus and of Rama and Krishna. For example, the birth of both Jesus and Krishna was signified by a star and took place in the middle of the night whilst an evil king was asleep.[14] Christians often say that Jesus was a historical person whereas Rama and Krishna were mythological. This, however, is to overstate the case. There probably are historical persons behind the stories of Rama and Krishna, but in the remote past. There are also mythological elements in the story of Jesus. Even so, the historicity of Jesus - even if details of his life are much disputed - is of great significance to Christians whereas there is in Indian thought a certain indifference to the historical. Vivekananda said the power of the gospel was independent of it having actually happened. 'It does not matter at all whether the New Testament was written within five hundred years of his birth, nor does it even matter how much of it is true.'[15] Gandhi too said that he did not care whether the crucifixion was historically true; it was truer than history. The Indian scholar A. D. Pusalker has said that 'an ordinary Hindu is never concerned with the historicity of Krishna; to investigate the problem is a sacrilege to him.'[16]

DIVINITY

To many Hindus 'divinity' is supreme holiness or goodness not another order of being. Pöhlmann recounts that two gurus told him that God was incarnate 'in my mother and every human being.'[17] Gandhi said 'If a man is spiritually ahead of us we may say that in a special sense he is the son of god, though we are all children of God. We repudiate the relationship in our lives, whereas his life is a witness to that relationship.'[18] Keshub Chandra Sen told his listeners that Christ was already in them. 'The holy Word, the eternal Veda dwells in every one of us. Go into the depths of your own consciousness, and you will find this indwelling Logos, the Son of God, woven warp and woof, into your inmost soul. Whatever in you is good and holy is the Son ... None can reach Divinity except through the character and disposition of the Son inherent in him.'[19]

It is not surprising, therefore, although it is often a shock to Westerners that some Hindu spiritual teachers are regarded as divine. Sai Baba (b. 1926), a spiritual guide with miraculous powers, is regarded by some of his followers as a manifestation of God. It was also interesting on a recent visit to the Brahma Kumaris World Spiritual University at Mount Abu to see that the founder Dada Lekh Raj, whose spiritual name is Prajapita Brahma, and who died in 1969, is treated almost as divine and as an embodiment of the god Siva. In India there are swamis who say of themselves, 'I and the Godhead are One' and to whom disciples come just for *darshan* - to sit in the presence of the holy person. Some Hindus class Jesus amongst the great seers who realized oneness with the Absolute. They think that when Jesus said 'I and the Father are One,'[20] he was describing an Advaitic experience of identity.

Only Son of God

Although in India Jesus is often spoken of as an *avatar*, some Christians have avoided the term because it seems to accommodate Jesus to Hindu presuppositions and may obscure the Christian claim that Jesus was unique or the *only* Son of God. This affirmation, however, is a problem for most Hindus and for some Indian Christians.

The distinguished Protestant theologian Stanley Samartha, who was Director of the Sub-Unit on Dialogue of the World Council of Churches, wrote in strong terms in his *One Christ, Many Religions* of the negative consequences of an exclusive claim in a multi-religious society. First, he says, it divides people into 'we' and 'they', the 'saved' and 'unsaved' and this hinders building a sense of national community and may be one reason why, in much of India, Christians are on the margin. Secondly, it makes co-operation among religious communities on social problems almost impossible. Thirdly, because Christianity and Hinduism have worldwide connections, any tensions within Indian society easily become internationalized and thereby heightened. Fourthly, Samartha maintains, exclusive claims raise serious theological questions. For example, what happened to the millions of people who were born before Jesus. Again, to emphasize that God's saving love is *only* revealed in Jesus seems to go against belief that God is the Creator, Sustainer and Redeemer of all humanity.[21]

Earlier in the book, Samartha suggests that the rejection of exclusivism is deeply embedded in Indian thought. Hindus speak of a unity of religions and their non-contradictoriness. Because of the basic differences in humankind, they regard it as natural and inevitable that there are religious differences. People are born into a particular religious community and tradition because of its suitability to their spiritual development, which is itself controlled by the laws of *karma*. God attracts a believer to the path that is right for him or her.[22]

This sense of an all-embracing unity is common in Indian religions. Jainism holds that because of the indeterminate nature of Reality, different viewpoints are possible and that none can claim final knowledge of the truth - which brings us back to the pervading sense of Mystery. The *Advaita* or 'non-dual' teaching that pervades much of Hinduism has a vision of a grand unity that holds together diversities in harmony.

Samartha therefore argues that whilst the classical creeds expressed Christian belief in terms of Greek philosophical thought, they are not the only way in which God's revelation in Jesus Christ may be spoken of and indeed are often unhelpful in an Indian context. The Gospel needs to be expressed in terms of Indian thought and the ways of thinking of other cultures. For India, the Christian message should include a sense of Mystery and a freedom from propositional theology.

Samartha also complains that some popular Christian devotion has become almost a Jesusolatry - worship of Jesus alone. In orthodox Christian thinking, as he says, Jesus is not the sum of the Godhead, rather the believer goes with Jesus to the Father. It has also been said that Jesus is wholly God but not the whole of God.

Samartha, further, criticizes what he calls 'a helicopter Christology', in which Christ as Saviour is suddenly brought in from the West. He contrasts this with a 'bullock-cart Christology', which starts from below - touching the unpaved roads of Asia.[23]

Samartha suggests that it is better to think of Jesus in terms of 'divinity' rather than 'deity'. 'It is one thing to say that Jesus of

Nazareth is divine,' he writes, 'and quite another thing to say that Jesus of Nazareth is God.'[24] Samartha quotes two New Testament scholars as saying, 'the God present in Jesus is God himself. It is not that Jesus in his own being is identical with the God who is present in him.'[25] Samartha insists that Jesus' primary concern was not with his own status but with the coming Kingdom of God and that this concern is relevant to all people.

Some modern Western Christological thinking seems to come close to Samartha's views and the attitude of some Hindu writers about Jesus. Orthodox Christian theology begins with God who becomes man. Liberal Christian thinkers tend to start with the real human being, Jesus, who lived in first-century Palestine. They see in the perfection of his humanity, for example in his total self-giving, a window on to God. The Scottish theologian Donald Baillie, in his influential book *God was in Christ*, tried to explain the incarnation in terms of the paradox of grace. The essence of this, he wrote, 'lies in the conviction which a Christian man possesses that every good thing in him, every good thing he does, is somehow not wrought by himself but by God.'[26] God, as it were, acts through the believer. Baillie suggested that 'this paradox of grace points the way more clearly and makes a better approach than anything else in our experience to the mystery of the Incarnation itself; that this paradox in its fragmentary form in our own Christian lives is a reflection of that perfect union of God and man in the Incarnation on which our whole Christian life depends, and may therefore be our best clue to the understanding of it.'[27] The union of Jesus with the Father is in this way seen more as one of total obedience and moral union rather than as ontological or a union of being.[28]

In my recent book *Christian-Jewish Dialogue: The Next Steps* I suggested that 'there was nothing un-Jewish in thinking that a great man had been signally honored by God in being taken up to heaven, in being given a role in the final judgement of the world and in being recognized as Messiah or Son of God. To the first believers, the term "Son of Man" probably implied Jesus' moral obedience to the Father.'[29] I also refer to James Dunn's argument that to call Jesus 'Lord' was evidently not understood in earliest Christianity as identifying him with God. Dunn says that 'what the first Christians seem to have done was to claim that the one God had shared his lordship with the exalted Christ.[30] Paul applied to Jesus language elsewhere applied to divine Wisdom (1 Cor. 8:6). He also spoke of God's glory being made visible in the face of Jesus Christ (2 Cor. 4:6) a term used in the Bible of the appearance of God in human form, sometimes called the angel of the Lord.'

Like Samartha I do not see the creeds as immutable, but as historical documents pointing to the central Christian experience of God's love in Jesus Christ. No one Christology is adequate, we need Christologies that try to convey the significance of Jesus to Hindu or Jewish or Muslim friends as well as Liberation and Feminist Christologies.

The Christian claim is that in Jesus we are met by God. Using the term *avatar* of Jesus may be helpful for some Hindus, for others it may suggest that Jesus is just one more intermediary whereas the Christian conviction is that in Jesus they have seen 'the glory of the One and Only, who came from the Father, full of grace and truth.'[31] In Jesus, I believe I have been met by the Living God who offers forgiveness and loving acceptance. All Christologies are at best inadequate attempts to convey the wonder of divine grace. As we share our experience and gladly hear the experience of others, we shall not compete about titles but join together in a chorus of praise to the one God who loves us all. Dialogue, as has been said, should be telling each other our beautiful names for God.

Once again, I resonate with words of Fr Bede Grifiths, who

wrote,

> I believe that the Word took flesh in Jesus of Nazareth and in him we can find a personal form of the Word to whom we can pray and to whom we can relate in terms of love and intimacy, but I think that he makes himself known to others under different names and forms. What counts is not so much the name and the form as the response in the heart to the hidden mystery, which is present to each one of us in one way or another and awaits our response in faith and hope and love.[32]

---

[1] H. Staffner, *The Significance of Jesus Christ in Asia*, Gujarat Sahitya Prakash, Anand, 388 001, 1985.

[2] H. Staffner, *The Significance of Jesus Christ in Asia*, Gujarat Sahitya Prakash, Anand, 388 001, 1985, p. 13.

[3] M. Gandhi, *The Message of Christ*, p. 3.

[4] M. Gandhi, *What Jesus Means to Me*, 1959, p. 18.

[5] Quoted from D. C. Scott, *Keshub Chandra Sen*, Christian Literature Society, Madras, 1979, pp. 198 ff. especially p. 200 and 217.

[6] R. S. Sugirtharajah indicates different ways in which some Indian thinkers have tried to incorporate Jesus into the thought forms of Hinduism: Ram Mohan Roy saw Jesus as a Supreme Guide to human happiness; Keshub Chandra Sen saw Jesus as a true *yogi* and divine human; Vivekananda saw Jesus as *Jivanmukta* one who has attained liberation while alive; Rabindranath Tagore saw Jesus as the Son of Man, seeking the last, the least and the lost; Gandhi saw Jesus as the supreme *Satyagrahi*, lover and fighter for truth; Swami Akhilananda saw Jesus as the *Advaitin,* one who has realized his destiny with Brahman/God; Radhakrishnan saw Jesus as the mystic Christ. Sugirtharajah lists the pioneering efforts of Indian Christians to see Jesus in an Indian context: K. M. Banerjee saw Jesus as *Prajpati*, Lord of creatures; Brahmobandhav Upadhyaya saw Jesus as *Cit*, (Consciousness); A. J. Appasamy and V. Chakkarai saw Jesus as Avatara, Incarnation; Chenchiah saw Jesus as *Adi Purusha*, and *Shakti* (power/ strength); and S. Jesudasan saw Jesus as Eternal *Om* (logos).

[7] Vivekananda, 'Christ the Messenger' in *Selections from Swami Vivekananda*, Advaita Ashram, 3rd edition 1957, p. 324.

[8] M. Gandhi, *Christian Missions*, 1941, p. 112.

[9] H. G. Pöhlmann, *Encounters with Hinduism*, SCM Press, 1996, p. 72.

[10] *Bhagavad Gita* 4, 8.

[11] Ayodhya in 1992 was the scene of bitter conflict between some Muslims and Hindus after some Hindus destroyed the mosque that was built on the site of a temple dedicated to Rama.

[12] *Oxford Dictionary of World Religions*, p. 795.

[13] See further the lecture by E. G. Parrinder, *The Significance of the Bhagavad-Gita for Christian Theology*, Dr William's Trust, 1968.

[14] Matthew 1:18-25; Luke 1:26-38 cp. *Bhagavata purana*, x, 3. See further O. N. Mohammed in *Asian Faces of Jesus*, ed. R. Sugirtharajah, p. 10.

[15] Vivekananda, 'Christ the Messenger' in *Selections from Swami Vivekananda*, Advaita Ashram, 3rd edition 1957, p. 326. See also M. Braybrooke, *Together to the Truth*, CLS, Madras, 1971, pp. 81-84.

[16] A. D. Pusalker, *Studies in the Epics and Puranas*, Bharatiya Vidya Bhavan, Bombay, 1955 p. 49, quoted by Samartha, p. 127.

[17] H. G. Pöhlmann, *Encounters with Hinduism*, SCM Press, 1996, p. 39.

[18] M. Gandhi, *Christian Missions*, p. 113.

[19] Quoted from D. C. Scott, *Keshub Chandra Sen*, Christian Literature Society, Madras, 1979, pp. 237-40.

[20] John 10:30.

[21] S. J. Samartha, *One Christ - Many Religions*, Orbis, Maryknoll, New York, 1991, p. 102.

[22] S. J. Samartha, *One Christ - Many Religions*, Orbis, Maryknoll, New York, 1991, p. 81.

[23] S. J. Samartha, *One Christ - Many Religions*, Orbis, Maryknoll, New York, 1991, p. 115.

[24] S. J. Samartha, *One Christ - Many Religions*, Orbis, Maryknoll, New York, 1991, p. 118.

[25] R. Fuller and P. Perkins, *Who is This Christ*, Fortress Press, Philadelphia, 1983, p. 8.

[26] D. M. Baillie, *God Was in Christ*, Faber and Faber, 1947, 1961 edition, p. 117.

[27] D. M. Baillie, *God Was in Christ*, Faber and Faber, 1947, 1961 edition, p. 117.

[28] See further A. Race, *Inter-faith Encounter*, SCM Press, 2001, chapter 4, especially pp. 76f., where Race distinguishes between a constitutive and a

representative Christology.

29 M. Braybrooke, *Christian-Jewish Dialogue: the Next Steps*, SCM Press, 2000, p. 74, but see the whole of chapter seven.

30 J. Dunn, *The Partings of the Ways*, SCM Press, p.191.

31 John 1:14.

32 Quoted by J. B. Trapnell, *Bede Griffits: A Life in Dialogue*, State University of New York Press, 2001, p. 153 from B. Griffiths, 'In Jesus Name', *The Tablet*, April 1992.

A NEW VIEW OF SCRIPTURE

The title page of the standard version of the Bible in Kannada, the language of the southern Indian state of Karnataka, with a literary history of about one thousand five hundred years, describes the Bible on the title page as 'the True Veda,' *Satya Veda*. The 1865 edition was printed in England, but when an edition was printed in India in 1951, the title page was unchanged. The implication was that the Bible was true and the scriptures or Vedas of the Hindus were false. Commenting on this, Stanley Samartha writes, 'To Christians it is astonishing that neighbours of other faiths also have written scriptures. The notion that the Bible is 'true' scripture and all other scriptures are 'false' is so stamped in the mind of many Christians that any discussion on scriptural authority becomes almost impossible.'[1]

Quite quickly as I began to read Hindu and other scriptures, I found passages that were 'inspiring'. What do I mean by inspiring, which is a vague phrase? Perhaps some passage which kindles my love of God and lifts my heart towards heaven. The poet Samuel Taylor Coleridge early in the nineteenth century suggested that the divinity of the Bible rested not 'in the infallibility of its statements, but in its power to evoke faith and penitence and hope and adoration.' He agreed that other books were inspiring, but not as much so as the Bible.[2] John Hick as early as 1973, in his *God and the Universe of Faiths*, quoted from prayers from a number of religions to show that in these 'we meet again and again the overlap and confluence of faiths.'[3] A growing number of people have by now found inspiration in the sacred scriptures of the world and have been willing to join together in prayer with members of different religions.[4]

This, however, implies a new view of the authority of scripture. The traditional Christian belief was that the Bible was literally the word of God, as it were, dictated to the evangelists and other authors. This traditional view was challenged in the nineteenth century but it can still be controversial even today to question the authority of scripture. At the beginning of the week in which I wrote this chapter *The Times* had a headline, 'Canon is banned for saying Bible is not the word of God.' A senior clergyman is reported as having said in a sermon that 'the elevation of the Bible to close on divine status has done more damage to the Christian message than all the slings and arrows of the sceptics. The Bible helps to point to the Word of God [the Logos] but it is not the word of God.'[5]

Traditionally, the divine authorship of the Bible was thought to ensure that it was free from error. This accounts for the ecclesiastical opposition to Charles Darwin's work on evolution and to the arguments of critical biblical scholars, which implied that not all statements in scripture were factually correct. Further, revelation was thought of in propositional terms as true statements about God. H. L. Mansel in his 1858 Bampton Lectures, for example, said that the Bible supplied 'regulative truths.' F. D. Maurice, a professor at King's College, London in contrast argued that revelation was participation in the very life of God.[6] Likewise, William Temple, Archbishop of Canterbury from 1942 to 1944, said 'that what is offered to man's apprehension in any specific revelation is not truth concerning God, but the living God Himself'.[7] Revelation is personal experience of the graciousness of God. Scripture, therefore, has a secondary authority - it points beyond itself to the self-expression of God in Jesus Christ. This means that historical inaccuracies are less important. Biblical writers communicate their experiences of God so that the reader can make those experiences his or her own. John, towards the end of his Gospel, writes, 'These things are written that you may believe that Jesus is the Christ, the Son of God, and that by believing you may have life in his name.'[8]

My early studies of Hinduism suggested that a similar change has been taking place in the Hindu view of the authority of the Vedas - indeed it was this study that helped me recognize the change in Christian thinking. Although the various orthodox schools of Hindu philosophy have different views about the nature of Vedic revelation, they accept the authority of the Vedas and claim that their thinking is based on these scriptures. The Vedanta school, for example, says its source is God, but also affirms that the Veda is eternal, which suggests that the Veda is free from historical conditioning and is therefore infallible. Some modern Hindu writers, however, take a different approach. Debendranath Tagore (1817-1905), leader of the Brahmo Samaj, found himself in disagreement with the Upanishads about the nature of the self's relationship to the Ultimate. He therefore rejected the infallibility of the scriptures. It was agreed in the Samaj that 'the Vedas, the Upanishads and other ancient writings were not to be accepted as infallible guides, that reason and conscience were to be the supreme authority and the teachings of the scriptures were to be accepted only insofar as they harmonized with the light within us.'[9] The inner light became the authority of the Samaj. 'I came to see,' said Debendranath, 'that the Pure Heart filled with the light of intuitive knowledge - this was its basis. Brahma reigned in the pure heart alone ... The rishi of old ... records his experience, "The pure in spirit enlightened by wisdom sees the Holy God by means of worship and meditation." (Mundaka III, 1-8). These words accorded with the experience of my own heart, hence I accepted them.'[10] Dr S. Radhakrishnan, however, adds that, 'The rishis are not so much the authors of the truths recorded in the Vedas as the seers who were able to discern the eternal truths by raising their life spirit to the plane of the universal spirit.'[11]

This change of perspective in both Christianity and Hinduism means that the scriptures, instead of being an infallible authority which tells us what to do and to believe, become as it were spiritual guide-books to help us on our journey towards God. In our reading of them, we are enriched and corrected by the insights of thousands of other people who have been inspired by them. Our own experience of God confirms them as authentic and authoritative.

Can we say that any one scripture is more authoritative or inspiring than another? I do not see that one can do this on objective or independent grounds. The acceptance of a scripture as authoritative goes with adherence to a faith community. W. Cantwell Smith says that 'On a close enquiry, it emerges that being scripture is not a quality inherent in a given text, or type of text, so much as an interactive relation between the text and a community of persons.'[12] It is the relationship to a community of faith that may make it difficult for a person of one faith to treat scriptures of another faith with the same authority as he or she accords to the scriptures of the faith community to which she or he belongs. Even so, other scriptures may also be a way in which God speaks to Christians.

It is worth noticing that different communities of faith have different understandings of the authority of scripture. 'To most Hindus,' writes Stanley Samartha, 'the primary authority lies in that which is *heard* rather than in what is *remembered* and written down. To the Buddhists scripture has an *instrumental* authority, like that of a boat that helps one to cross the river, but which, after reaching the other shore, becomes unnecessary.'[13]

Nonetheless, can a member of one religious tradition find inspiration in the scriptures of another? The Sikh scriptures, the

Guru Granth Sahib or Adi Granth, which was originally compiled by the fifth Guru, Guru Arjan in 1604 - in the same year as work began on the Authorized or King James Version of the Bible - contains devotional hymns by Hindu and Muslim poets and saints as well as by the Gurus. For example, poems by Kabir, the mystic and religious reformer, are included - as in these lines:

Whoever by the Master's guidance wakes, is noble.
Many are the tasks performed by this body
Saith Kabir: To the Name Divine be devoted[14]

Christians include the Hebrew Scriptures in their Bible. In India, at some Christian ashrams there may at the Eucharist be readings from Hindu scriptures as well as from the Bible. Should the reader at the end of the passage say, 'This is the Word of the Lord,' as would normally be said after a reading from the Bible?

A Consultation on this subject, held in Bangalore in 1988, made the following points. First, God's Word is a greater reality than the scriptures themselves. God has spoken in different manners to a variety of human histories. Secondly, selective use of other scriptures is in tune with the Christian principle of selective use of biblical texts. Many churches have chosen readings for particular Sundays and do not read the whole Bible in public worship. Thirdly, just as Christian scriptures are the gift of the Word of God offered by the Christian community as a record of its faith, so other scriptures can be considered also as a gift of the Word of God offered to Christians by members of other religious traditions. Nonetheless, fourthly, the Consultation recognized a phenomenon called 'the historical divergence' of God's Word, whereby the Word of God of one community is enshrined by the cultural modes of a particular community.[15]

The fourth point was a recognition of the specific character of each religious tradition. Other scriptures need to be understood in their own context, not manipulated to confirm Christian beliefs, as so often Christians have misused the Hebrew Scriptures or Old Testament. Yet the context of Christian worship in which a passage from another scripture is read may suggest a particular meaning or interpretation for the chosen passage. But then no text from scripture is univocal. Any verse is subject to different interpretations, depending on the background and outlook of the reader.

The Consultation recognized that reading from other scriptures during Christian worship may well be beneficial, provided it is not done to criticize those to whom the text belongs nor misused out of context to support Christian claims. It can help us see that God speaks to every faith community. The same is true of occasions when people of different faiths come together for prayer and the reading of passages from the scriptures of the world.[16]

In our personal devotions also we can be enriched by the sacred texts of the world. Raimundo Panikkar in his great collection of Vedic texts for modern man or woman called *The Vedic Experience*, whilst recognizing that the Vedas are 'linked for ever to the particular religious sources from which they historically sprang', also says that the Vedas are a monument of universal religion and therefore of deep significance for all people.[17]

To recognize that every scripture is a gift of God for all humanity follows logically from recognizing that each religion draws its inspiration from the One Divine Reality. Scriptures are sacred treasures held in trust by one community, but for the benefit of all people.

This further suggests that, whilst we are primarily nourished spiritually by the scriptures and teachings of the community of which we are a member, we can find inspiration in the writings of other traditions. This also means that a new approach to theology, sometimes called 'global theology' or 'comparative theology' becomes possible.

Traditionally theology has been reflection by members of one faith community on the meaning and implications of texts or scriptures, which are held to be authoritative. It has been an essentially confessional discipline. Now, however, as the scriptures of the world have been translated into English and many other western languages, we can draw upon the insights of the scriptures of the world for our theological reflection. Indeed, some twenty years ago, the distinguished scholar Wilfred Cantwell Smith wrote 'henceforth the data for theology must be the data of the history of religions. The material on the basis of which a theological interpretation shall be proffered, of the world, man, the truth, and of salvation - of God and His dealings with His world - is to be the material that the study of the history of religion provides.'[18]

The exciting possibility awaits us of seeing how this knowledge can increase and deepen our understanding of the Divine Mystery, which can never be fully grasped by one tradition alone.

---

[1] S. Samartha, *One Christ - Many Religions*, Orbis, 1991, p. 58 and note on p. 164.

[2] S. T. Coleridge, *Aids to Reflection* and *Confessions of An Enquiring Spirit*, see A. R. Vidler, *The Church in an Age of Revolution*, Penguin, 1961, pp. 79-82.

[3] J. Hick, *God and the Universe of Faiths*, Macmillan, 1973, p. 141.

[4] See *All in Good Faith*, ed. J. Potter and M. Braybrooke, World Congress of Faiths, 1997.

[5] *The Times*, 23.7.2001, p. 3.

[6] See further A. R. Vidler, *The Theology of F D Maurice*, SCM Press, 1948, pp. 178-182.

[7] W. Temple, *Nature, Man and God*, The Gifford Lectures, University of Glasgow, 1935, p.322.

[8] John 20:31.

[9] D. Tagore, *The Autobiography of Maharshi Debendranath Tagore*, Calcutta, no date. Introductory chapter by R. Tagore, p. 5.

[10] D. Tagore, *The Autobiography of Maharshi Debendranath Tagore*, Calcutta, no date, pp. 161-2.

[11] S. Radhakrishnan, *An Idealist View of Life*, 1932.

[12] W. C. Smith, *What is Scripture*, SCM Press, 1993, p. 9.

[13] S. Samartha, *One Christ - Many Religions*, Orbis, 1991, p. 62.

[14] *Sri Guru Granth Sahib*, Translated by Gurbachan Singh Talib, Punjabi University, Patiali, 1994 edition, Vol 4, pp. 2411-2.

[15] The report of one group at a conference on 'Sharing Worship' held at the National Biblical Catechetical and Liturgical Center at Bangalore in 1988. See *Sharing Worship*, ed. P. Puthanangady, National Biblical Catechetical and Liturgical Centre, Bangalore, 1988, pp. 747-750.

[16] See further *All in Good Faith*, ed. J. Potter and M. Braybrooke, World Congress of Faiths, 1997, chapters 2 and 3.

[17] R. Panikkar, *The Vedic Experience*, Darton, Longman and Todd, 1977, p.4, but see the whole introductory section.

[18] W. C. Smith, *Toward a World Theology*, Macmillan, 1981, p. 126. See also my *Faith and Inter-faith in a Global Age*, CoNexus Press and Braybrooke Press, 1998, chapters 9 and 11.

KARMA AND REINCARNATION

'There may be parallels between Jesus Christ and Krishna and Rama, but is there any place for forgiveness in Hinduism?' is a question that Christians sometimes ask. The cross speaks to Christians of a God who takes the initiative in forgiving sinners, but in the basic Buddhist and Hindu cosmology, there seems to be no place for human repentance and divine forgiveness. This at least is the opinion of my good friend Joe Elder. Writing in the book *Exploring Forgiveness*, he says, 'Central to the Buddhist-Hindu cosmology is the law of karma. According to the law of karma, every virtuous act is rewarded and every sinful act is punished in an inexorable manner similar to the laws of physics. The punishments and rewards might happen in this life or in subsequent lives but they *will* happen. There is no process of repentance or forgiveness that can affect the inevitability of the punishments and rewards.'[1]

The belief that we have all lived before and that the conditions of our present life are a direct consequence of our previous lives is widespread amongst Hindus. Karma and rebirth are said to solve one of the great problems of life. The question, writes R. K. Tripathi, who taught at Banaras Hindu University, is 'How is it that different persons are born with an infinite diversity regarding their fortunes in spite of the fact that God is equally good to all? It would be nothing short of denying God to say that he is whimsical. If God is all-goodness and also all-powerful, how is it that there is so much evil and inequality in the world? Indian religions relieve God of this responsibility and make our karmas responsible.'[2]

Does this mean that our present life is predetermined by our past? At one conference of the World Congress of Faiths someone told us of a boy in India who was very ill and who needed to be flown to London for very special treatment. We were asked to contribute to the cost of his fare. I recall one Sikh suggesting that perhaps his illness was his karma and it was not for us to interfere. Some sociological studies of how the doctrine of karma is actually used in daily life suggest, however, that it does not inhibit a parent seeking a cure for a child who is ill. If that child were to die, then at that point the idea of karma might be introduced to try to ease the sense of loss, just as someone in the West might say 'the child was spared further suffering.' Karma, like the Christian doctrine of original sin, seems to me not so much to explain the inequalities of life as to acknowledge them. To blame karma is to blame one's own past actions and this should encourage a person not to act badly again. In the same way, Christian teaching about sin is intended to lead to repentance and a change of behaviour.

Usually the doctrine is interpreted to leave some place for personal freedom and responsibility. The philosopher Dr S. Radhakrishnan wrote, 'The cards in the game of life are given to us. We do not select them. They are traced to our past karma, but we can call as we please, lead what suit we will, and as we play we gain or lose. And there is freedom.'[3] Gandhi used the doctrine of karma to suggest that people could help to shape the future by their present behaviour. Rather than being backward looking, karma should encourage us to take care about how we shape our future.

Even in the Hindu scriptures the law of karma is not in full control. According to the strict law of karma, there is no scope for expiation or repentance, as everyone has to experience the consequences of their sinful actions for the sin to be destroyed. Yet the attainment of *moksa* or realization takes a person out of *samsara*, the cycle of rebirth, and beyond the realm where karma operates. Further, the scriptures also provide for rituals to expiate wrongdoing. Many of the Dharma-Sastras written during the classical period of Hinduism discuss various sins and moral transgressions along with their respective atonements. The many penances, said to have been enumerated by the ancient lawgiver Manu, form the core of the ancient Indian criminal code. The *Manusmrti* says that 'An evil-doer is freed from his evil by declaring (the act), by remorse, by inner heat, by recitation (of the Veda) and, in extremity, by giving gifts. The more a man of his own accord declares the wrong that he has done, the more he is freed from that wrong like a snake from his skin.' (11, 228-231)[4]

In the devotional bhakti traditions, the repetition of the divine name, often on a rosary (*japa*), was the most popular way of wiping out wrongdoing and its effects. In several theistic traditions karma is God's instrument and subject to God's control, rather than an inexorable law. In several traditions there is reference to God's mercy. In the *Gita*, repentance born of love and faith wipes away all sin and no one who comes to God with a humble heart fails to win salvation. 'No one who worships me with loyalty-and-love is lost to Me,' says Lord Krishna, 'For whosoever makes me his haven, base-born though he may be, yes women too and artisans, even serfs, theirs is to tread the highest way.' (9, 31-34) Krishna is the Good Herdsman in quest of the worst sinner who has not repented: 'However evil a man's livelihood may be, let him but worship Me and serve no other, then he shall be reckoned among the good indeed, for his resolve is right.' (9, 30) Faith in Lord Krishna, transcends the normal requirements of *dharma*. 'For knowledge of the Veda, for sacrifice, for grim austerities, for gifts of alms a reward is laid down: all this the athlete of the spirit leaves behind.' (8, 28) Right at the end of the *Gita*, Krishna reassured Arjuna that he need not worry about the law but should trust Krishna's love and grace, 'Give up all things of law, turn to Me, your only refuge, [for] I will deliver you from all evils; have no care.' (18, 66)

In the hymns of the Tamil saints, both Saivite and Vaishnavite, there are many appeals to God for mercy and expressions of gratitude to God for forgiveness. The great South Indian saint Yamunacarya (918-1040), who was a devotee of the god Vishnu, cried out, 'I have committed thousands of sins. I am helpless and come for refuge to your sacred feet. By your grace, make me yours.'[5] The great Saivite poet Manikavacakar sang of God's love for humankind and rejoiced in God's mercy:

You bestowed on me a grace undeserved by me
and enabled this slave's body and soul
to joyfully thaw and melt with love.
For this I have nothing to give in requital to You,
O Emancipator pervading the past,
the future and every thing!
O infinite primal Being ... [6]

There is even a debate between those who think the devotee depends entirely on God's grace, like a kitten picked up by its mother, and those who think some human effort is also required, like a baby monkey who has to cling on to its mother.

Even if the law of karma does not have the iron grip sometimes assumed by outsiders, it does emphasize moral responsibility and that every action has its effect. Jesus said a person will reap what they sow. Sadhu Sundar Singh, who converted to Christianity from his childhood Sikhism, gave an internalized explanation of the law of karma. He believed firmly in retribution, but regarded this as brought about by an *internal* necessity or inevitable degeneration of the personality, which brings its own punishment and renders a person incapable of attaining the life of heaven. It is not a punishment by God, for, as the Sadhu said, 'Jesus Christ is never annoyed with anybody.'[7] Bad actions corrupt the personality. There is an echo here of passages in John's Gospel where it is said that God does not judge anyone but that people judge themselves by refusing to come to the Light. Sundar Singh affirms that the Love of God is always available to intervene and correct the retributory process of karma, but not by an 'external' forgiveness or mere remission of the penalty. God works by changing the heart and thereby curing the moral disease which is the root of sin.

I think it can be seen that bad actions corrupt the character and that people bring judgement upon themselves. People who tell a lie often have to tell more lies to cover up the original untruth. Tragically too, evil behaviour can inflict lasting damage on other people's personalities - as for example in the loss of self-respect in those who are the victims of violence and sexual abuse. Our behaviour has moral consequences both for others and for ourselves. This does not, however, explain the unfairness of life.

That, most Hindus say, requires a belief in rebirth. Although the Lingayats and some other Hindu groups reject this belief, it is widespread in Indian thought. Philosophical and empirical reasons are given for this belief. It is assumed that the soul by its nature is eternal, which was also the view of the third-century Christian thinker Origen (c. 185-c. 254) - although in *Advaita* philosophy from the standpoint of realization the individual soul is not other than the Universal Soul. It is further argued, as we have seen, that the unfairness of life can only be explained if there are many lives. The person born handicapped or destitute is paying the price for the sins of a past life. In some teaching this rebirth may be in other worlds or it may be as an animal. The doctrine may be given a future reference. The great twentieth-century Hindu thinker Sri Aurobindo, in his *Life Divine*, has an evolutionary framework and sees the whole process leading the soul to full awareness. 'The true foundation of the theory of rebirth', he wrote, 'is the evolution of the soul, or rather its efflorescence out of the veil of Matter and its gradual self-finding.'[8] Other modern Hindu writers also have a forward-looking emphasis. The Saiva Siddhantin scholar Dr Devasenapathi wrote, ' "From a savage to a saint," is not that a perfect description of the increasing purpose in all history and the meaning of it all?'[9] Dr T. M. P. Mahadevan, a distinguished Advaitin philosopher at Madras University, also insisted that the belief that the universe goes through a recurring pattern of four ages or *yugas*, does not imply that history just repeats itself. The theory of four ages, he said, 'does not mean that the time process is cyclical but rather it is like a spiral.'[10]

I have found this concept helpful in my own thinking. Recently, when we were staying at the Brahma Kumaris Spiritual University at Mt Abu, Dadi Prakashmani, the Administrative head, invited our group for a conversation. During this she asked us whether we believed in reincarnation. My answer was that I pictured every soul on a journey towards God, but I did not know whether that journey involved more than one life in this world. Various beliefs were combined in this statement. The first is my belief that God's love for every person is unending - that God will never rest until every soul responds to that divine love. This is in Christian terms the doctrine of 'Universalism' - that in the end every soul will be saved and come into the full presence of God. I do not believe in hell - other than in the sense of the misery human beings inflict on themselves and each other by their cruel and selfish behaviour. I am aware that very few people are ready for the vision of God at the end of this life and I have never been at ease with the Protestant view that our eternal destiny is determined by life in this world alone. The Catholic doctrine of Purgatory allows for progress beyond death towards God, but has often been seen as a punishment. It should be understood in terms of the word 'purge'.

It is, in my thought, part of the process by which we move from our self-centredness to becoming centred on God. The disciplines and trials of this and other lives are remedial. They prepare us for full communion with God.[11]

Such an approach gives us a picture of all human beings moving towards God, but the Love of God has to be freely accepted. As Paramahansa Yogananda, the founder of the Self-Realization/Yogoda Satsanga of India said, 'God will not tell you that you should desire Him above all else, because he wants your love to be freely given, without "prompting". That is the whole secret in the game of this universe. He who created us yearns for our love. He wants us to give it spontaneously, without His asking. Our love is the one thing God does not possess, unless we choose to bestow it. So, you see, the Lord has something to attain: our love. And we shall never be happy until we give it.'[12] There is no compulsion, only an eternal yearning in the heart of God. Such pictures of progress are inevitably time-bound. All time is present to God. But some pictures of God are more fitting than others and they can colour our behaviour towards other people. Even if in traditional thinking it is God who sends people to hell, God's faithful have been tempted to anticipate God's judgement! Too often those with different beliefs have been demonized. A belief that all people will be saved encourages a remedial or restorative approach to the treatment of criminals rather than one which stresses punishment and retribution.

In our journey towards God, do we visit planet Earth more than once? I do not know - certainly there are many experiences that I would like to have had, but many I am glad to have been spared. The empirical arguments for rebirth include the newly born infant's instinct to suck which, it is said, must have been learned in a previous life. Infant geniuses, it is claimed, remember skills learned in an earlier incarnation. There are those who claim to recall incidents from a previous life. Many people have a sense of *déjà vu*, of going to a place for the first time but finding it is already familiar.

There may be other explanations for these experiences. One difficulty with the theory of reincarnation is that most of us do not remember our previous lives. Is it moral for us to be punished in this life for a wrongdoing that we cannot recollect?[13] Yet our adult character and behaviour are shaped by childhood happenings which we do not recall - other perhaps than during psychoanalysis. The question of personal identity is far from simple.

My picture of our future destiny does not entirely fit with either traditional Christian or Hindu teaching, but draws on insights from both - and from other religions. This is perhaps an example of the possibility, suggested at the end of the last chapter, of what W. Cantwell Smith calls a 'Global theology' or Keith Ward has spoken of as 'Comparative theology'. In our thinking about the most profound existential and theological issues we can draw on insights of the great traditions. This, however, implies a new perspective, whereby we see theological thinking not as reflection on intellectual propositions once and for all revealed by God, but as a never ending quest for a fuller understanding of the Divine Mystery that we never fully apprehend. As Jesus said, 'the Spirit of truth will guide you into all truth.'[14]

---

[1] J. Elder, 'Expanding Our Options' in *Exploring Forgiveness*, ed. R. D. Enright and J. North, The University of Wisconsin Press, Madison, 1998, p.158. Admittedly Joe Elder adds that some Hindus and Buddhists, such as the Dalai Lama, see close parallels between the reframing dynamics of Christianity and Judaism and those endorsed by Buddhism.

[2] R. K. Tripathi, *Problems of Philosophy and Religion*, quoted by J. Hick, *Death and Eternal Life*, Collins, 1976, p. 302.

[3] S. Radhakrishnan, *The Hindu View of Life*, 1927, p. 75.

[4] *The Laws of Manu*, ed. W. Doniger and B. K. Smith, Penguin Books, New Delhi, 1991, p. 273, quoted by G. L. Beck 'Fire in the Atman: Repentance in Hinduism', in *Repentance: A Comparative Perspective*, ed. A. Etzioni and D. E. Carney, Rowman and Littlefield Publishers, Lanham, 1997.

[5] V. Narayanan, *The Way and the Goal: Expressions of Devotion in the Early Sri Vaisnava Tradition*, Institute for Vaishnava Studies and Center for the Study of World Religions, Harvard University, Washington DC, 1987, p. 66.

[6] Quoted in *The Lotus Prayer Book*, ed. Swami Satchidananda, Integral Yoga Publications, Yogaville, Virginia, 1986, p. 101.

[7] Quoted by B. H. Streeter and A. J. Appasamy, *The Sadhu*, Macmillan, 1922, p.157.

[8] S. Aurobindo, *The Problem of Rebirth*, vol. 16, p. 86, quoted by J. Hick, *Death and Eternal Life*, Collins, 1976, p. 321.

[9] Devasenapathi, *Towards the Conquest of Time*, Miller Lectures, Madras University, 1962, p. 39.

[10] T. M. P. Mahadevan, *Time and the Timeless*, Miller Lectures, Madras University, 1958, p. 250 and for 1962, p. 37. See further M. Braybrooke *Together to the Truth*, CLS, Madras, 1971, pp. 136ff.

[11] It will be seen that I have considerable sympathy with the position reached by John Hick in the final chapters of *Death and Eternal Life*. Collins, 1976.

[12] Paramahansa Yogananda, *How Can You Talk With God*, Self Realization Fellowship, Los Angeles, 1957.

[13] See further J. Hick, *Death and Eternal Life*, Collins, 1976, chapters 16 and 17.

[14] John 16:13.

Ahisma

Vegetarianism

'Do we have to have vegetarian meals all the time?' complained some of the tour group that I led to Gujarat early in 2001. As a vegetarian myself I was delighted, but had not wanted to impose my preference on the rest of the party. But Gujarat is an area of India that is much influenced by the Jain religion. Jains emphasize the importance of *ahimsa* or non-violence so the restaurants at most of the hotels in the smaller towns are vegetarian and there is also no alcohol available. Indeed, before climbing the Jain holy mountain of Shatrunjaya with its amazingly beautiful temples, we had been warned that we must not wear anything made of leather.

Jains believe that every centimetre of the universe is filled with living beings, some of them minute. All deserve to live and evolve and humans have no special right to supremacy. To kill any living being has adverse karmic effects. It is difficult to avoid doing some violence to other living creatures, but Jains refrain from eating after sunset to avoid unknowingly swallowing insects. Monks and nuns will cover their mouths with cloths to avoid inhaling an insect and some will brush the path in front of where they walk to avoid treading on any living being. As the *Akaranga Sutra* says, 'All breathing, existing, living, sentient creatures should not be slain, nor treated with violence, nor abused, nor tormented, nor driven away. This is the pure unchangeable, eternal law.'[1]

Jainism, with its teaching of *ahimsa*, had a profound influence on Mahatma Gandhi, although he was himself a Hindu. Gandhi was born in Gujarat, at Porbandar, on the Western coast of India and our tour group visited the house where he was born and grew up. Gandhi applied the practice of *ahimsa* to the struggle against the British for India's independence. This and his influence on Martin Luther King, the champion of black civil rights in the USA, had a profound effect on the history of the last century.

I am now a vegetarian and a pacifist and certainly India influenced me, as it has influenced many others, in this evolution. Like Jains, many Hindus are vegetarian - especially most Brahmins, unless they have adopted a Western style of life. At Madras Christian College, as is common in India, there were separate 'veg' and 'non-veg' dining rooms. After a time, I changed to the vegetarian option, partly because the food was not so hot and spicy and this suited me better. It was also cheaper, as I was not finding it easy to manage on the scholarship, which was set at the rates for Indian students and I needed European luxuries such as sunscreen cream! Even if my motivation was mixed, I felt a certain liberation at not being dependent on the slaughter of other living beings. On my return to England, I reverted to Western norms. It was not until my daughter, at the age of sixteen and after seeing a programme on factory farming, declared that she would never eat meat again, that I began to become a practising vegetarian.

I am not a proselytizing vegetarian and recognize that it is a personal choice. A number of Christians, including some Church Fathers and the founder of Methodism, John Wesley, were vegetarian, but the eating of meat is accepted in the Bible as a consequence of the Fall. I recognize that complete non-violence is impossible but I try to be as non-violent as possible. I object to many of the practices of factory farming and the exploitation of animals and recognize that the excessive consumption of meat in the Western world uses up a lot of grain, which could be made available for those who are always hungry. I am aware, however, that to some extent vegetarianism is in the West an affluent middle-class option and that if I were a starving beggar I would eat whatever scraps were thrown at me.

I do also recognize a hierarchy of living beings in that I regard human life as more valuable than animal life and would not oppose *essential* medical experiments on animals, although I am not persuaded that all experiments are essential. But if driving a car I could not avoid hitting either a dog or a child, I would try to avoid hitting the child. Gandhi himself said, 'I have no feeling in me to save the life of those animals which devour or cause hurt to man.' He was not opposed to killing mosquitoes and other disease carriers.[2]

Christianity has been subject to much recent criticism for its acquiescence - even encouragement - of the exploitation of nature, said to be based on the verse in Genesis where God gave man 'dominion over the fish of the sea, and over the fowl of the air, and over the cattle and over all the earth.' (Genesis 1:26 *AV*) Yet, the verse begins, 'Let us make man in our image, after our likeness ...' Human rule of the animal creation and the natural world should mirror what I believe to be God's loving care for all life. Much of the nineteenth- and twentieth-century exploitation of the animal and natural world derives more from the Enlightenment and especially the teaching of the philosopher René Descartes (1596-1650) than from Christian teaching. Descartes regarded animal behaviour as mechanical and he dismissed the opinions of Montaigne and others who attributed understanding and thought to animals. Animals, he wrote, 'act naturally and mechanically, like a clock.'[3] Christian teaching came to echo these Renaissance views. An early version of the *Catholic Dictionary* (1884) under the heading 'Animals, Lower' has this entry: 'As the lower animals have no duties ... so they have no rights ... The brutes are made for man, who has the same right over them which he has over plants or stones.' Admittedly the *Dictionary* says man should not take pleasure 'directly in the pain given to brutes,' but this is not out of a concern for animal suffering but because such action 'brutalizes his own nature.'[4] Even today, some argue for ecological programmes for the sake of humanity's future rather than from an awareness of the sacredness of the Earth.

In recent years there has been an increasing recognition of the interdependence of all life and a new respect for the animal and natural world. It would be an interesting study to see to what extent this has resulted from the influence upon the West of Asian religions, although in the USA, Native American spirituality has also been influential. Certainly E. F. Schumacher, the author of *Small is Beautiful,* was much influenced by Buddhist teaching and devotes a section of his book to Buddhist economics.[5]

Although there is much cruelty in the treatment of animals in the Indian subcontinent, as elsewhere in the world, all the Indian religions teach a sense of oneness with nature and a reverence for life. The cow, which is regarded as sacred and wanders freely in most parts of India, is a symbol of this. Mahatma Gandhi said '"Cow Protection" to me is one of the most wonderful phenomena in all human evolution; for it takes the human being beyond his species ... Man through the cow is enjoined to realize his identity with all that lives ... "Cow Protection" is the gift of Hinduism to the world.'[6] I am sure I am not alone in having been made more sensitive to these issues by the influence of Hinduism, Buddhism and Jainism.

PACIFISM

Various influences also have led me become a Christian pacifist, although perhaps Peter Bishop's term 'pacificist', which I will explain below, is more appropriate. When I first met her, Mary, who was to become my wife, was secretary of the Cambridge branch of the Fellowship of Reconciliation, which was founded as a Christian pacifist organization early in the twentieth century. So, to spend time with her, I would sometimes accompany her to Fellowship of Reconciliation meetings. This encouraged me to think more about issues of war and peace.

It was, however, studying some of the writings of Mahatma Gandhi and his teaching on *ahimsa* and *satyagraha* that helped me to see the practical possibilities of non-violence, which were also used to such good effect by Martin Luther King, who was himself deeply influenced by Gandhi. In turn, this helped me to see the teaching and example of Jesus in a new light and recognize the radical nature of his call to love the enemy.

Gandhi once defined the Hindu creed as the 'search after truth through non-violent means.'[7] The word *ahimsa* that characterizes his teaching is more positive than the usual translation 'non-violence' suggests. The Sanskrit word *himsa* means to injure, or destroy, or kill. Gandhi took *himsa* to mean not only the harming of living things but also 'hurt by every evil thought, by undue haste, by lying, hatred, by wishing ill to anybody.'[8] So *ahimsa*, in its positive form, he said, 'means the largest love, the greatest charity. If I am a follower of *ahimsa*, I must love my enemy or a stranger to me as I would my wrong-doing father and son.'[9] Gandhi also used the term *satyagraha*. 'Truth (*satya*) implies love,' he explained, 'and firmness (*agraha)* engenders and, therefore, serves as a synonym for force. I thus began to call the Indian movement *Satyagraha,* that is to say the Force which is born of Truth and Love or non-violence.'[10] *Satyagraha* was a non-violent method of opposing wrong.

Peter Bishop stresses that *satyagraha* is not pacifism. 'Of course it was influenced by the *ahimsa* of Jainism and Buddhism and of Gandhi's native Gujarat; it was influenced by the ideal of the Sermon on the Mount, as Gandhi understood that part of the New Testament; it was influenced by Ruskin and Thoreau and Tolstoy; it was influenced by the idea of disinterested service found in the *nishkama karma* [doing your duty without fear or favour] of the *Gita*. But *satyagraha* was nevertheless Gandhi's own concept. He adopted the word *satyagraha* in order to avoid 'pacifism', which he regarded as a negative term describing a negative response to oppression.'[11] Passive resistance seemed like the weapon of the weak, whereas *satyagraha* 'postulates the conquest of the adversary by suffering in one's own person.'[12] The aim was not so much to defeat the opponent but to convert him. Gandhi was convinced that truth and right was on his side and that eventually the opponent would come to recognize this. This would lead to reconciliation rather than conquest. Victory by violence, he believed, only breeds resentment and sows the seed of future violence. As Martin Luther King put it, 'The old law of an eye for an eye leaves everybody blind. It is immoral because it seeks to humiliate the opponent rather than win his understanding; it seeks to annihilate rather than to convert. Violence is immoral because it thrives on hatred rather than love. It destroys community and makes brotherhood impossible. It leaves society in monologue rather than dialogue. Violence ends by defeating itself. It creates bitterness in the survivors and brutality in the destroyers.'[13]

If, as Jesus said, you pray for those who persecute you,[14] you do not forget their fellow humanity even while you oppose what they say and do. There is a certain compassion or concern for the enemy as well as for allies. Much civil disobedience today, which may look in part to Gandhi for its inspiration, lacks this concern for the conversion of the opponent and even when it is successful creates the potential for future conflict. Hannah Arendt, in her book *On Violence*, suggested that the power that 'springs up whenever people get together and act in concert' and violence are opposites.[15]

There have been many examples of this 'people power' from the mothers of the 'Disappeared' who bore witness during the Argentine junta's reign of terror, to the throngs of Filipinos marching behind statues of the Virgin Mary up to President Marcos' tanks and the mass protests that led to the collapse of Communism in much of Eastern Europe. The influence of Gandhi has been immeasurable. As Martin Luther King said, 'If humanity is to progress, Gandhi is inescapable.'[16]

Gandhi believed that the power of Love is the same as the power of Truth and that it was as much a law of the universe as the law of gravitation. 'I have simply tried in my own way,' he said, 'to apply the eternal truth to our daily life and problems.'[17] He learned the lesson, he said, from the non-violence of his wife. 'Her determined resistance to my will on the one hand, and her quiet submission to the suffering my stupidity involved on the other hand, ultimately made me ashamed of myself and cured me of my stupidity in thinking I was born to rule over her; and in the end she became my teacher in non-violence.'[18]

Yet for all his advocacy of *satyagraha*, Gandhi did not rule out violence in all circumstances. This is what Peter Bishop means by a 'pacificist' - someone who puts the emphasis on making peace rather than refusing to use any violence. In 1920 Gandhi wrote, 'I do believe that, where there is only a choice between cowardice and violence, I would advise violence.'[19] *Ahimsa* was not the non-violence of the weak. His opposition to violence seems to have increased, but he agreed with the need for an armed police force in an independent India, although he hoped for a State where eventually a police force would not be necessary.[20]

The history of the Sikhs is perhaps a warning that non-violence is not possible in every situation. The early Gurus rejected the use of violence. When the fifth Guru was arrested by the Emperor Jehangir he remained calmly meditating on God as he was tortured by heat. But thereafter Sikhism took measures to protect itself and the sixth Guru built up a Sikh army. The tender-hearted seventh Guru was a pacifist who never used his troops against the

Mughals and taught the Sikhs to feed anyone who came to their door. The ninth Guru was executed by the Emperor Aurangzeb for opposing his attempts forcibly to convert Hindus and Sikhs to Islam. Gobind Singh, the tenth Guru, inaugurated the Khalsa, a band of disciplined warriors who resisted Mughal oppression and defended freedom of religion. Most Sikhs would maintain that self-defence and protection of the weak and poor may require the use of force.

A commitment to non-violence seems to me to involve the recognition that it is both an ideal for which we aim while it is also the means to that ideal. There may be situations where we have to choose the least violent option. A United Nations Peace Keeping Force to monitor a cease-fire is better than a civil war, but the members of that UN Force may have to shoot in self-defence.

Gandhi had a holistic view of society. He advocated women's emancipation; he taught the dignity of physical labour and encouraged cottage industries; he attacked abuses of the caste system and called the outcastes '*Harijans*' or 'children of God'. A non-violent society is only possible if there are far-reaching changes to the structural violence of its political and economic practices. Indeed the roots of violence go back to childhood and the parenting we received. As Charlene Spretnak points out in her book *States of Grace*, 'Studies of the childhoods of Nazi leaders have found that they were often made to feel inherently unlovable and undeserving and were granted only a harsh, extremely conditional acceptance; beatings were common. In contrast, a study of rescuers in Nazi Europe found that, unlike the control group in the study, the rescuers had almost no memories of being punished gratuitously and had rarely been punished physically. There was generally one parent or parental figure who, in the child's eyes, embodied very high standards of ethical behaviour. The child witnessed and experienced a life lived with the truth of interconnectedness.'[21]

The more non-violent we become in all our behaviour and attitudes, the more we contribute to the creation of a non-violent society. This is perhaps why it was right to deal with questions of vegetarianism and of war and peace in one chapter. *Ahimsa*, which is part of the traditional culture of Gujarat, has through its most famous son, Mahatma Gandhi, offered the world a way to reverse the growing spiral of violence, sadly evident in so many societies.

---

1 Akaranga Sutra, Fourth Lecture, First lesson, in *Sacred Books of the East*, ed. F. M. Müller, vol. XXII, Jaina Sutras part 1, Clarendon Press, Oxford, 1884, p. 36.
2 *Harijan*, 5.5.46.
3 Descartes, *Philosophical Letters*, translated and edited by A. Kenny, Oxford University Press 1970.
4 *The Catholic Dictionary*, 13th edition, 1884, quoted by L. G. Regenstein, *Replenish the Earth*, SCM Press, 1991, p. 114. Regenstein's book is a good source of information on this subject.
5 E. F. Schumacher, *Small is Beautiful*, Harper and Row, 1973.
6 Quoted in *Hinduism*, ed. J. R. Hinnells and E. J. Sharpe, Oriel Press, 1972, p. 120. No reference given.
7 M. Gandhi, *Young India*, 10.4.1924.
8 M. Gandhi, *From Yeravda Mandir: Ashram Observances*, 3rd edition, Navajivan Publishing House, 1945.
9 M. K. Gandhi, from a letter in *Modern Review*, Oct. 1916.
10 M. K. Gandhi, *Satyagraha in South Africa*, Tanam Press, New York, 1983, pp. 109-110.
11 P. D. Bishop, *A Technique for Loving: Non-Violence in Indian and Christian Traditions*, SCM Press, 1981, p. 83.
12 *The Selected Works of Mahatma Gandhi*, Ahmedabad, 1968, Vol. 3, p. 157. See also P. D. Bishop, *A Technique for Loving: Non-Violence in Indian and Christian Traditions*, SCM Press, 1981, p. 52.
13 *The Words of Martin Luther King*, ed. C. Scott King. Newmarket Press, New York, 1983, p. 73.
14 Matthew 5:44.
15 H. Arendt, *On Violence*, Harcourt Brace and World, New York, 1970, p. 56.
16 *The Words of Martin Luther King*, Ed C Scott King, Newmarket Press, New York, 1983, p. 71.

[17] M. K. Gandhi, *Towards Non-Violent Politics and the Relation of Constructive Work to Ahimsa*, Sarvodaya Prachuralaya, Thanjavur, 1969, p. 3. Quoted by C. Spretnak in her valuable discussion in *States of Grace*, HarperSanFrancisco, 1991, chapter 2.
[18] Quoted by G. Ashe, *Gandhi: A Study in Revolution*, William Heinemann, 1968, p. 182.
[19] M. Gandhi, *Young India*, 11.8.1920.
[20] M. Gandhi, *Harijan*, 1.9.1940.
[21] C. Spretnak, *States of Grace*, HarperSanFrancisco, 1991, p. 77. She refers to A. Miller, *For Your Own Good*, Farrar Straus Giroux, New York, 1984 and S. Griffin, 'The Child and the Shape of History', *Creation*, Vol. 4, no 6 Jan/Feb. 1989, p. 22, for studies of the childhood of Nazis and S. P. Oliner and P. M. Oliner, *The Altruistic Personality: Rescuers of Jews in Nazi Europe*, The Free Press, New York, 1988.

Poverty and Caste

'How do you cope with the poverty?' was a question that Mark Tully, who was for several years the BBC correspondent in Delhi, was often asked by his visitors. 'Ask the rickshaw wallahs,' was his reply.

It is, of course, the destitute who suffer the affliction of hunger and disease, but the poverty and the beggars are bound to have an impact on any visitor from the affluent West. In South India, meals are sometimes served on the leaves of a plantain or banana tree. After the meal, these are collected and thrown on the rubbish dump. I recall my shock, soon after first arriving in India, at seeing some hungry young children picking over these leaves looking for a few grains of rice. Yet, in fact, confrontation with the poverty in parts of India only underlines the injustice of our world of which we have no excuse for being ignorant.

Westerners are usually advised not to give to beggars, who can be persistent and aggressive. It is suggested that some children are deliberately maimed to make them more pitiable. On the other hand, by refusing we may harden our heart and cut off the bonds of human sympathy. When one does give, it seems to me important to look into the eye of the beggar - if he or she is not blind - and to see there a fellow human being.

A litany used at Calcutta Cathedral helps to convey what life is like for a beggar:

Poverty is

- a knee-level view from your bit of pavement;
a battered, upturned cooking pot and countable ribs,
coughing from your steel-banded lungs, alone, with your face to the wall;
shrunken breasts and a three year old who cannot stand;
the ringed fingers, the eyes averted and a five-paise piece in your palm;
smoking the babus' cigarette butts to quieten the fiend in your belly;
a husband without a job, without a square meal a day, without energy, without hope;
being at the mercy of everyone further up the ladder because you are a threat to their self-respect;
a hut of tins and rags and plastic bags, in a warren of huts you cannot stand up in, where your neighbours live at one arm's length across the lane;
a man who cries out in silence;
nobody listening, for everyone's talking;
the prayer withheld,
the heart withheld,
the hand withheld; yours and mine
Lord teach us to hate our poverty of spirit.[1]

City of Joy,[2] the title of a well known book about Calcutta, is a reminder of the generosity of many who are very poor and Mary and I have known the wonderful welcome and hospitality of those whose homes are very simple. Poverty of spirit may be as deadly as physical poverty and the affluence of the West brings its own problems. But these considerations are no reason to allow so many children to die young or for the lives of those children who survive to be stunted by malnutrition.

A concern for the poor has throughout been part of my ministry, especially when we were in the Medway Towns. There I took an active part in work for Christian Aid and in the beginnings of what has become the World Development Movement - for poverty requires structural change to our economic and political systems as well as generous giving. Exposure to the poverty of India and other parts of the world have made many people aware of the deep economic injustices of the world and uneasy with lavish displays of luxury.

Yet the real motive for compassion should not be guilt but thanksgiving. I recall in one parish suggesting at Christmas time that an extra place should be laid at the festive table to remind us of the hungry and that the equivalent of the cost of one person's meal should be donated to Christian Aid. One parishoner commented. 'You are not going to spoil Christmas as well as Harvest Festival, are you, by making us feeling guilty?' Compassion should flow from thanksgiving. If we are aware of the wonder and beauty and richness of life and recognize that all is a gift of God then we shall want all people to share in God's bounty. There is a Jewish saying that we shall be judged for every legitimate pleasure that we did not enjoy. I believe God wants us to enjoy the good things of life. If we recognize that these are God's gifts then we shall not claim possession of them nor be reluctant to share them.

In serving the poor we also serve the Lord. To quote the prayer of the workers at Mother Teresa's orphanage at Caluctta, 'Dearest Lord, may I see you, today and everyday, in the person of your sick, and whilst nursing them, minister unto you. Though you hide yourself behind the unattractive guise of the irritable, the exacting, the unreasonable, may I still recognize you, and say, "Jesus my patient, how sweet it is to serve you."' In the parable of the sheep and the goats, Jesus, who has been called 'the man for others' said, 'What you do to the least of my brothers and sisters you do to me.' [3]

To recognize the Lord in the marginalized and disadvantaged is to question the priorities of many religious institutions and to be uneasy with religious triumphalism. As Rabindranath Tagore wrote,

> Leave this chanting and singing and telling of beads!
> Whom dost thou worship in this lonely dark corner of a temple with doors all shut?
> Open thine eyes and see thy God is not before thee!
> He is where the tiller is tilling the hard ground and where the path maker is breaking stones ... Put off thy holy mantle and even like him come down on the dusty soil!
> ... Meet him and stand by him in toil and in sweat of thy brow.[4]

There is a similar emphasis in the Sikh religion. From the beginning, Sikh Gurus rejected the caste system and affirmed that every person is precious to God. The common kitchen or *langar* is open to everyone regardless of caste, creed, colour or sex. There are no special seats. Rich and poor sit side-by-side on the ground without distinction. Sometimes it is the men who serve the food to women. For in the teaching of the Gurus, as in the teaching of Jesus, women are of equal dignity in the eyes of God. If there has been discrimination, it has been cultural and not religiously sanctioned. The Gurus also did not look down on manual work.

Guru Har Rai, the seventh Guru, not only taught Sikhs to feed anyone who came to their door, but

> 'to do service in such a way that the poor guest may not feel he is partaking of some charity but as if he had come to the Guru's house which belonged to all in equal measure. He who has more should consider it as God's trust and share it in the same spirit. Man is only an instrument of service: the giver of goods is God, the Guru of us all.'[5]

On our first visit to the Baha'i temple in Delhi we were amazed by its beauty, but on leaving the taxi drove through some of the worst slum shanti towns that we have ever seen. This is not a criticism of the Baha'is, but a question about the financial priorities of most religious groups and as a parish priest one of my responsibilities has been to raise money to help preserve some of England's historic village churches. Indeed awareness of the poor puts a question to all our priorities. Especially in my inter-faith work, I have tried to keep in mind Gandhi's 'Talisman'.

I will give you a Talisman.
Whenever you are in doubt,
or when the self becomes too much with you,
apply the following test:
'Recall the face of the poorest
and weakest man whom you may have seen
and ask yourself if the step you contemplate
is going to be of any use to him.'
Will he gain anything by it?
Will it restore him to a control
over his own life and destiny?
In other words, will it lead to Swaraj
for the hungry and spiritually starving millions?
Then you will find your doubts
and your self melting away.

International inter-faith conferences may seem a long way from the burdens of the poor, but I have hoped that the coming together of religions in understanding and co-operation would help to reduce violence, which is a cause of so much suffering and poverty, and unite religions in active work to help the most needy.

This hope was born in me one very hot day as I went for the first time with other students from Madras Christian College to help at a Leprosy Clinic. One of the other students was a Roman Catholic from Sri Lanka and another was a Muslim from Hyderabad. The doctor, who gave his services, was dressed in a traditional *dhoti* and as, a devotee of the god Siva, had ash on his forehead. Despite our differences, we were together in the service of the afflicted. Even so, I had to wrestle with myself to overcome some of the inherited prejudices about leprosy. Would I catch it by touching the children who had it?

CASTE

At times religious teaching has been used to reinforce the fear of leprosy and many Westerners have a justifiable anger at the caste system and practice of untouchability. The caste system is very complex and is by no means the only cause of widespread poverty which some Indians would see primarily as a legacy of imperialism.

Defenders of caste speak of it as a system of mutual responsibility. 'The underlying principle' of caste, wrote T. M. P. Mahadevan, 'is the division of labour. Originally the castes were professional and subsequently became hereditary.'[6] Similarly, Swami Harshananda told Dr Pöhlmann that caste 'has a social function because a person's caste gives protection, security and an identity, so that one knows where one belongs.'[7] The stylized system of the scriptures speaks of Brahmins, who are priests, Ksatriya or warriors, Vaisya or merchants and of Sudras or manual labourers, although the reality is far more complex.

The origins of caste, which is a Portuguese term, are lost in obscurity. In part it was a result of various waves of conquest, but it also reflects concerns for purity and the fear of pollution. To enter the presence of God, as in biblical times, a person had to be ritually pure. Pollution is inevitably involved in bodily functions: eating, excretion, perspiration, menstruation, birth, death. Some temples have notices forbidding a woman during her monthly period from entering its precincts. Pollution, in some traditions, can be removed by bathing and looking at the sun. The priests, because of their role, were careful to avoid pollution, but by so doing cut themselves off from other castes and would not eat with or marry someone of a lower caste. Often religious sanctions were used to reinforce their caste privileges.

There are also those known traditionally as outcastes, sometimes called Harijans or Dalits, with whom members of the higher castes avoided all physical contact. Gandhi, who defended the theory of caste, said, 'I consider untouchability to be a heinous crime against humanity ... I know of no argument for its retention and I have no hesitation in rejecting scriptural authority of a doubtful character in order to support a sinful institution.'[8] After Indian Independence, untouchability and caste discrimation were abolished by law. Pandit Nehru and his colleagues wanted to create a social democracy in India. Long inherited attitudes and customs, however, cannot be abolished by legislation and in much of Indian society, especially the villages, casteism is still endemic. In some villages the casteless are refused the use of the village well and not allowed entry to the temple.

Some Christians, indeed, reject any dialogue with Hinduism because it condones casteism and discrimination. This was brought home to me at a meeting in preparation for a great inter-faith gathering, Sarva Dharma Sammelana, which was held at Bangalore in 1993. I had asked a well known Hindu from a very high caste to chair the event. This alienated some of the Christians who were committed to Dalit theology and who have adapted liberation theology to their situation. Not only do they reject any dialogue with Hinduism, because it condones the caste sytem and has been the cause of so much injustice in India, they also reject 'classical Indian (Christian) theology' of, for example Appasamy and P. Chenchiah, because, they say, it is completely shaped 'by the Brahminic tradition of Hinduism.' [9]

It is difficult for an outsider to comment on the situation. As

Pöhlmann comments, 'Aren't there also class distinctions and castes in our Western society?'[10] Christian children used to be taught to sing

The rich man in his castle,
The poor man at his gate
God made them high and lowly
And ordered their estate.[11]

Further, some Christians in India retain some caste attitudes, for example in the choice of a husband or wife.

This is why the the exchange of the peace, which I first encountered in the the Church of South India liturgy, is so powerful a symbol. At the Communion service, everyone is asked to greet each other and wish them the peace of the Lord, regardless of caste or social status.

Some of the Hindus most active in inter-faith dialogue, such as Swami Agnavesh, are very critical of casteism and discrimination. There is, however, always a danger of dialogue glossing over social abuse, although paradoxically, inter-faith activity often does not help to unite religions, but rather it creates an alliance amongst people of different faiths who are committed to social justice and change.

Although many Hindus keep to traditional ways, the twentieth century saw vast changes in Indian life. Economic and sociological reasons may be primarily responsible for this as well as the emphasis on scientific ways of thinking, which concentrate on this world and how it works. Science has given to human thought an autonomy so that it does not rely upon the divine for explanations. Several thinkers have contributed to these changes. For example, the influential thinker Sri Aurobindo (1872-1950), when he retired to his *ashram,* claimed that he was not abandonning the political struggle but was seeking a spiritual basis for 'efficient action'. Indeed, already in 1913 the missionary scholar J. N. Farquhar noted that 'the life of India is dominated by the future, by the vision of the brilliant happy India that is to rise as a result of the united toil and self-sacrifice of her sons.'[12] In Buddhism too, which Albert Schweitzer spoke of as a world-negating religion, there is a growing movement of 'Socially Concerned Buddhists.'

The change in Hinduism is not just in theory but in practice. Most large Hindu movements have extensive social, medical and educational work and could be said to have copied the methods of Christian missionaries. Swami Vivekananda, noting that his guru Sri Ramakrishna said that 'An empty stomach is no use for religion', encouraged the Ramakrishna Mission to develop educational, medical and relief work.

A striking example of Hindu social commitment is the Kashi ashram in Florida, founded by Ma Jaya Sati Bhagavati. Ma grew up in poverty in a Jewish family in Brooklyn, New York. In 1972, her spiritual awareness was awakened by a vision of Christ, who told her, 'Teach all ways, for all ways are mine.' Her spiritual journey led her to the teaching of the Hindu saint Sri Nityananda of Ganeshpuri and to the Guru Neem Karoli Baba.

Ma has dedicated her life to work for world peace and the relief of human suffering. She has been outspoken in challenging the prejudice with which victims of Aids and HIV infection have often been treated. Many sufferers, including children, have been cared for at the ashram, whose members dedicate themselves to social service. Ma has also been outspoken in her support for the people of Tibet.[13]

The growing emphasis on social service flows from a recognition that, in Rabindranath Tagore's words, God is as likely to be met in the person of the poor as in a temple. Mahatma Gandhi said, 'The immediate service of all human beings, *sarvodaya,* becomes necessary ... because the only way to find God is to see him in his creation and to be one with it.'[14] Similarly, Swami Vivekananda, before he set out for the World's Parliament of Religions, dedicated himself at Kanniyakumari, on what is now known as Vivekananda's rock, to 'My God, the afflicted; My God, the poor of all races.'[15]

I was glad, therefore, that when in 1993 we went to India to celebrate the centenary of the first World Parliament of Religions, our very first visit was to Vivekananda's rock. It was a reminder to me that the coming together of people of faith should be an offering of service to bring help and hope to the poorest people of our planet.

---

1 Litany from Calcutta, quoted in *Another Day,* edited by John Carden, Triangle/SPCK 1986, p. 112.

2 D. Lapierre, *City of Joy*, Random House, 1985.

3 Matthew 25:40.

4 R. Tagore, *Gitanjali*, 11, Papermac, Macmillan 1986, p. 8.

5 Quoted from Dr Gopal Singh, *A History of the Sikh People,* World Sikh University, New Delhi 1979, p. 257.

6 T. M. P. Mahadevan, *Outlines of Hinduism,* Chetana, Bombay 1956, 2nd edition 1960, p. 69.

7 Quoted by Horst Georg Pöhlmann, *Encounters with Hinduism,* SCM Press 1996, p. 56.

8 Quoted by T. M. P. Mahadevan, p. 75.

9 Quoted by Pöhlmann, p. 78 from A. P. Nirmal, 'Towards a Christian Dalit Theology' in *Heuristic Explorations*, 1990, p. 139ff.

10 *Ibid,* p. 57.

11 From the hymn 'All things bright and beautiful.'

12 J. N. Farquhar, *The Crown of Hinduism*, Humphrey Milford 1913, p. 149.

13 For further information contact the Kashi Foundation, 11155 Roseland Rd, Sebastian, Florida 32958 USA.

14 M. Gandhi, *Harijan.* Quoted by Bede Griffiths, *Christian Ashram,* Darton, Longman and Todd, 1966, p. 127.

15 Quoted by D. S. Sarma, *Hinduism Through the Ages,* Bharatiya Vidya Bhavan, Bombay, 1967, p. 64.

Conclusion

Service of a world in need requires more than help to individuals. It demands a transformation of world society that is based on the ethical and spiritual values of the world faiths. This is why a mystical awareness and social activism are linked together. John V. Taylor, a former Bishop of Winchester, wrote, 'The unique and authentic opening of the eyes by the Spirit of creativity within the heart of all things produces that double exposure by which what is and what might be are seen together in a single vision.'[1] Thomas Merton, in a paper given in Bangkok on the day of his death, said that the monk 'is essentially someone who takes up a critical attitude towards the contemporary world and its structures.'[2] Daniel Berrigan, a priest who was active in his opposition to the Vietnam War, went further. 'The time will shortly be upon us,' he wrote, 'if it is not already here, when the pursuit of contemplation will become a strictly subversive activity.'[3]

It is encouraging, therefore, that increasingly people of different faiths are beginning to address together the urgent issues that face humankind. The 1993 Parliament of the World's Religions was, to my mind, a turning point in inter-faith work. The question was no longer whether people of faith could or should meet together, but what could they do together for the benefit of the world. Of course some inter-faith activists had asked that long before.[4] There was, for example, in the eighties an Inter-faith Colloquium against Apartheid and there were various inter-faith gatherings on ecological issues as well as inter-faith prayer and work for peace, but the Parliament for a moment captured the attention of the world and sought to show, at a time of intense conflict in former Yugoslavia and of communal troubles in India, that religions need not be a cause of division but could unite on certain basic ethical teachings.

At the 1993 Parliament, most members of the Assembly signed a document called 'Toward a Global Ethic'. They agreed that a Global Ethic, based on the fundamental demand that every human being must be treated humanely, offered the possibility of a better life for individuals and a new global order. The document emphasized 'Four Irrevocable Directives':

1. Commitment to a culture of non-violence and respect for life.
2. Commitment to a culture of solidarity and a just economic order.
3. Commitment to a culture of tolerance and a life of truthfulness.
4. Commitment to a culture of equal rights and partnership between men and women.[5]

In the years since 1993, the Council for a Parliament of the World's Religions has attempted to see how these ethical demands can affect the life of our whole society. At the 1999 Cape Town Parliament 'A Call to Our Guiding Institutions' was issued. This invited those engaged in government, business, education, arts and media, science and medicine, intergovernmental organisations and the organisations of civil society, as well as those in positions of religious and spiritual leadership, to 'build new, reliable, and more imaginative partnerships towards the shaping of a better world.'[6] It was a call to find new ways to co-operate with one another and to reflect together on the moral and ethical dimension of their work. It was a pity that too few leading members of the Guiding Institutions were there, because dialogue now needs to be inter-disciplinary as well as inter-faith.

At the same time as the focus of much inter-faith activity has become more practical, those in positions of leadership in the political and economic spheres are both recognizing the importance of religion in shaping the modern world and acknowledging that there is a spiritual and ethical dimension to the major problems facing humankind. There is space only to give a few examples of this development.

Since 1993, UNESCO has held several conferences addressing the role of religion in conflict situations and at the 1994 conference in Barcelona issued a 'Declaration on the Role of Religion in the Promotion of a Culture of Peace'. UNESCO has established an International Inter-religious Advisory Committee and with the UN launched the year 2000 as 'the International Year for a Culture of Peace'.[7]

In 1998 a meeting on 'World Faiths and Development' was held at Lambeth Palace, London, jointly chaired by James D. Wolfensohn, President of the World Bank, and by Dr George Carey, the Archbishop of Canterbury. From this emerged World Faiths Development Dialogue. This has brought together two actors on the development scene, the religious communities and the multilateral development agencies, which until now have gone their own way with considerable mutual suspicion. Now the hope is to bring together those who possess expertise in technical issues and faith communities which stand closer than any others to the world's poorest people. Such a conscious step to forge an alliance should lead, in the words of Dr Carey and James D. Wolfensohn, 'to inspiration and learning among people from all sides and to ways of making some real changes in favour of those who most need them.'[8]

In 2001, for the first time, The World Economic Forum, an independent foundation that engages business, political and other leaders of society seeking to improve the state of the world, invited religious leaders to share in their deliberations on globalization. It was recognized that 'religious traditions have a unique contribution to offer ... particularly in emphasizing human values and the spiritual and moral dimension of economic and political life.'[9] In the same year, the 12th Anti-Corruption International Conference, which was held at Prague, for the first time included a panel - in which I was invited to participate - about the contribution of faith-based organizations to the struggle against corruption.

The most striking example of the new seriousness with which international decision makers are taking the contribution of faith communities was the historic Millennium World Peace Summit of Religious and Spiritual Leaders, which met in UN General Assembly Hall in August 2000. Partly because of the opposition of Communist countries, the United Nations has kept itself at some distance from faith communities, although religious NGOs have, for many years, made a contribution at certain levels, in particular to specialist agencies. The meeting, which issued a 'Commitment to Global Peace', was, therefore, of great symbolic significance.

Further, at national and local level in many countries there is growing emphasis on inter-faith understanding and practical co-operation, although in all too many places religious differences embitter existing conflict.

This co-operation is very important and the great suffering in our world makes it urgent. I wonder, however, if it will be sustained without a sense of human unity that the mystical vision inspires. Paul Knitter in his *One Earth, Many Religions* emphasizes the priority of 'the dialogue of action' in response 'to the widespread human and ecological suffering and injustice that are threatening our species and our planet'[10] but he recognizes that 'unless the voices of the mystic and the scholar are also heard, the conversation will lose its religious content or it will be turned into a tool for purposes that can only discredit all the participants.'[11] I felt that to some extent this happened at the UN Peace Summit. Some leaders seemed mainly interested in promoting their own religious tradition and there was little listening. I was also not sure whether the spiritual leaders were being enlisted to support the UN agenda or whether the UN was really open to critique and dialogue.

Further, the emphasis on the practical may allow faith communities to avoid the challenge to their traditional exclusivism which a mystic vision implies. The Hinduism from which I have learned teaches the spiritual oneness of all people, although too much of Hinduism today in India is caught up with communalism and political rivalries. That oneness, which springs from a sense of oneness with the Divine, inspires compassion and concern for all people and indeed for all living beings. As Hindu teachers sometimes say, 'Love your neighbour as yourself, because he is yourself.' Many of the great Hindu teachers of the twentieth century have emphasized that a mystic awareness should inspire practical service to the poor. Indeed the *Gita* teaches that 'when a person responds to the joys and sorrows of others as if they were his own, he has attained the highest state of spiritual union.' (6, 32).

The ancient Vedic tradition speaks of unity and compassion. It is appropriate to end this book with two prayers from the Hindu tradition that can be an inspiration to all people of faith.

O God, let us be united;
Let us speak in harmony;
Common be our prayer;
Common be the end of our assembly;
Alike be our feelings;

Unified be our hearts;
Common be our intentions;
Perfect be our unity.[12]

Let your soul lend its ear to every cry of pain
like as a lotus bares its heart to drink the morning sun.
Let not the fierce sun dry one tear of pain
before you yourself have wiped it from the sufferer's eye.
Rather, let each burning human tear fall on your heart
and there remain nor ever brush it off,
until the pain that caused it is removed.[13]

---

1 J. V. Taylor, *The Go Between God*, SCM Press 1972, p. 74.

2 Quoted by Kenneth Leech, *The Social God*, Sheldon Press 1981, p. 45.

3 *Ibid*, p. 53.

4 See *Stepping Stones to a Global Ethic,* ed. M. Braybrooke), SCM Press 1992.

5 *A Global Ethic: A Declaration of the Parliament of the World's Religions,* ed. Hans Küng and Karl-Josef Kuschel, SCM Press 1993.

6 'A Call to Our Guiding Institutions', Council for a Parliament of the World's Religions, Chicago 1999.

7 I am grateful to Dr Josef Boehle for permission to use this material from his as yet unpublished doctoral thesis for the University of Birmingham, 'Inter-religious Co-operation in a Global Age', pp. 63-91.

8 *World Faiths Development Dialogue, Exploring Dialogue,* A Report on Progress July 1998-December 2000, WFDD, 2001, p. 3.

9 Press Release issued by the International Council of Christians and Jews, 31.1. 2001.

10 P. F. Knitter, *One Earth, Many Religions,* Orbis, 1996, p. 13.

11 *Ibid,* pp. 155-6.

12 Quoted from the Vedas in *All in Good Faith*, ed. J. Potter and M. Braybrooke, World Congress of Faiths, 1997, p. 73.

13 Quoted from the Vedas in the *The Golden Thread*, ed. D. Boux, Shepheard-Walwyn and Gateway Books, 1990, p. 95.

Further Reading

There are many introductory books on Hinduism. Here is a brief selection:

Jeanne Fowler, *Hinduism: Beliefs and Practices*, Sussex Academic Press, 1997.

V. P. (Hemant) Kanitkar and W. Owen Cole, *Teach Yourself Hinduism*, Hodder Headline, 1995.

Klaus Klostermaier, *A Short Introduction to Hinduism*, Oneworld, 1996.

Kim Knott, *Hinduism: A Very Short Introduction*, Oxford University Press, 1998.

Swami Kriyananda, *The Hindu Way of Awakening*, Crystal Clarity, Nevada City, CA, 1998.

Julius Lipner, *Hindus: Their Religious Beliefs and Practices*, Routledge, 1994, (paperback 1998).

Bansi Pandit, *The Hindu Mind*, B and V Enterprises, Glen Ellyn, IL 60137, 1992.

There are also many books on Christian-Hindu dialogue. Here

again is a short selection:

Abhishiktananda, *Guru and Disciple*, (English translation Heather Sandeman), SPCK, 1974.

Roger Hooker, *Voices of Varanasis*, CMS, 1979.

Klaus Klostermaier, *Hindu and Christian in Vrindaban*, SCM Press, 1969.

Nirmal Minz, *Mahatma Gandhi and Hindu-Christian Dialogue*, CLS, Madras, 1970.

Horst Georg Pöhlmann, *Encounters with Hinduism*, SCM Press, 1996.

John Robinson, *Truth is Two Eyed*, SCM Press, 1979.

Stanley Samartha, *The Hindu Response to the Unbound Christ*, CLS Madras, 1974.

Hans Staffner, *The Significance of Jesus Christ in Asia*, Gujarat Sahitya Prakash, Anand, India, 1985.

M. M. Thomas, *The Acknowledged Christ of the Indian Renaissance*, SCM Press, 1969.

Vandana, *Gurus, Ashrams and Christians*, Darton, Longman and Todd, 1978.

There are many books by Fr Bede Griffiths. His writings are listed in Shirley Du Boulay's biography of him: *Beyond the Darkness*, Rider, 1998. Good ones with which to start are:

The Marriage of East and West, Collins and Templegate Publishers, 1982.

The Cosmic Revelation: The Hindu Way to God, Templegate Publishers, 1983.

GLOSSARY

Advaita, non-dual school of philosophy
Ananda, bliss, one of the characteristics of Ultimate Reality
atman, the self
Avatara, incarnation
Bhagavad Gita, the best known Hindu scripture
Brahma Kumaris, a modern spiritual movement
Brahman, Supreme Being, Ultimate Reality
Cit, consciousness, one of the characteristics of Ultimate Reality
darshan, a viewing of a god
dharma, the way of righteousness
Dharma-Sastras, law books
Durga, goddess, consort of Siva
Ganga, the sacred river of the north, personified as a goddess
Hanuman, monkey god
Japa, rosary
jnana yoga, the way of knowledge
Kali, goddess, with a terrifying aspect
karma, activity and its result
Krishna, avatar of Vishnu, worshiped as a god
Laksmi, goddess of wealth
lingam, phallic symbol, used as a symbol of the god Siva
Mahabharata, Hindu epic
mantras, a sacred syllable

Manusmrti, the laws of Manu
Moksa, release or liberation from ignorance and rebirth
Neti, Neti, not this, not that; Ultimate Reality can only be described in negative terms
nishkama karma, doing one's duty without fear or favour
Parvati, goddess, the wife of Siva
Radha, consort of the god Krishna
Rama, avatar of Vishnu, worshipped as a god
Ramayana, Hindu epic
Saivite, devotees of the god Siva
Sakti, energy, term used of the divine female power
samsara, the cycle of rebirth
Sarasvati, goddess of learning
Sat, Being, one of the characteristics of Ultimate Reality
satyagraha, truth-force
Sita, consort of Rama
Siva, one of the most widely worshipped gods
Theravadin, major school of Buddhism
Upanishads, Hindu scriptures
Vedas, Hindu scriptures
Vishnu, a very widely worshipped god; Krishna and Rama are his avatars
Visistadvaita, qualified non-dual school of philosophy

INDEX